GRADES 3-5

STEP UP
to Better Grades

For Classrooms, Small Group, and Individuals

by Robin S. Zorn Ed.S

8 Sessions That Teach Children Good Study Habits

INCLUDING 66 EXTENSION ACTIVITIES AND REPRODUCIBLE INTERACTIVE WORKSHEETS

youth light inc.

© 2016 by YouthLight, Inc. | Chapin, SC 29036

Layout and Design by Melody Taylor/GraphicSolutions, Inc.
Project Editing by Susan Bowman

Library of Congress Control Number: 2014942226
ISBN: 978-1-59850-160-5

10 9 8 7 6 5 4 3 2
Printed in the United States

⟨ DEDICATION ⟩

I would like to dedicate this book to all the school counselors, teachers, and school social workers who make a difference in the lives of children each and every day.

To know even one life has breathed easier because
you have lived – that is to have succeeded.
~ Ralph Waldo Emerson

⟨ ACKNOWLEDGEMENTS ⟩

I would like to acknowledge the following people for their support and guidance in the development of this book for without them this endeavor would not have been possible.

To my husband Bob for his unconditional love and support. Thank you for always believing in me and for holding down the fort while I dive into these adventures.

To my daughters, Annlen and Mary-Taylor, for continuing to inspire me to follow my dreams every day.

To my family and friends who remind me that all things are possible for those who have faith and believe.

To my partners, Merrill Baxley, who spent time reading and editing this book and Paige Price and Holly Rivas who have always been my biggest cheerleaders.

To all the staff members at Mason Elementary School and the school counselors in Gwinnett County, Georgia who continuously encourage me to be the best school counselor that I can be.

To Bob and Susan Bowman and the staff at Youthlight for guiding and encouraging me through my first publication. I could not thank you all enough.

To ASCA and GSCA for letting me present *STEP-UP to Better Grades* at conferences and for opening up opportunities for me to succeed.

Table of Contents

CD Contents

8 Parent Letters (one for each session)
5 Power Point Presentations to Supplement Key Lessons
ASCA Mindsets and Behaviors
All Reproducible Pages from Activities

Introduction

Overview of STEP-UP to Better Grades

As an elementary school counselor, I have been teaching study skills small groups for years like many school counselors do throughout the year. It wasn't until 2003 that I began thinking about making sense out of all the study skills habits that can be taught. For years I would focus on various skills from the needs assessment, but I often found that it was difficult for the students to remember the strategies and then apply them. That was when I created the acronym STEP-UP to help students remember key study skills habits.

Each letter in STEP-UP represents a word that describes a specific study habit or skill. The letter "S" stands for SPACE. This section focuses on having a more effective study space at home. The letter "T" stands for TOOLS. This section focuses on the tools that a student needs to help them stay organized. The letter "E" stands for ENDING. This section focuses on setting goals for completing your work. The first "P" stands for PAY ATTENTION which focuses on listening skills. The letter "U" stands for UNDERSTAND DIRECTIONS by following written and oral directions. And the last letter "P" stands for PRACTICE. This section shares different ways to study.

There are eight sessions in this book; one overview lesson, six lessons using each of the letters in STEP-UP, and a STEP-UP to Better Grades review lesson. By remembering what study skill each letter represents, students can then remember the study skills that will help them to be successful in school.

Benefits of this Program

- Students will remember the letters and what they stand for from year to year. This helps when teaching them in subsequent years and when working with individual students.

- In SST (Student Support Team) meetings, RTI (Response to Intervention) meetings, parent conferences, and teacher conferences it is easy to recall the study skills lessons you will cover by just remembering the letters. I have found this helpful when parents ask me what I cover in the study skills small groups or core curriculum lessons.

- This program can be easily taught by teachers, counselors, social workers or other school staff.

- Parents are encouraged to reinforce the lessons at home through parent letters.

Tips for Using this Book

Core Lessons and Activities

- Each letter has a Core Lesson. The Core Lessons teach the overall study skills habit and then the activities support it.

- Once you teach the core lesson you can choose as many activities to support that skill. For example, if your students are having a difficult time following directions, you may teach several lessons on the letter "U" (UNDERSTAND DIRECTIONS) by choosing several of the activities provided.

Small Groups

- You can teach STEP-UP to Better Grades for as many weeks as you need. If you find in your small group that you need to spend more time on a particular letter (habit) you can add additional activities to support that skill.

- You can work with students to master each habit by checking in with the teacher to see they are applying what they learned.

- Parent letters support each session and lets them know what was taught and provides suggestions on how to reinforce the skill at home.

- There is a pre and post-test that you can use to assess the students. These can be used for your small group perception data.

- You can modify the activity when it says, "divide the class" to make it work for small groups.

Classroom Lessons

- There are eight Core Lessons. Based upon the needs of your students and the amount of time you have, you can teach the Core Lessons and as many Activities that you would like to support that habit.

- To create a three lesson unit you can combine letters into one lesson. For example, you can teach the following for an Academic Unit:

Lesson1:

STEP-UP to Better Grades Pre-test

Brief overview of STEP-UP to Better Grades Curriculum

Letter "S" – SPACE Core Lesson key points. Touch on Do's and Don'ts from Activity 2.1

Letter "T" – TOOLS Core Lesson key points.

Activity 3.2 – What happened to my Grades (use the entire worksheet or put examples on the board if you are limited on time).

Lesson 2:

Review letters "S" and 'T."

Letter "E" – ENDING Core Lesson key points.

Choose a supporting Ending Activity

Letter "P" – PAY ATTENTION Core Lesson key points.

Choose a supporting Pay Attention Activity

Lesson 3:

Review letters "S," "T," "E," and "P."

Letter "U" – UNDERSTAND DIRECTIONS Core Lesson key points.

Choose a written or oral directions activity based on need

Letter "P" – PRACTICE Core Lesson key points.

Choose a supporting Practice Activity

STEP-UP Review

STEP-UP to Better Grades Post-test at a later time.

- In subsequent years you can review the Core Lessons because the students are familiar with the program and then choose different activities to teach for each letter.

- There is a pre and post-test that you can use to assess the students. You can use the results for your core curriculum perception data.

- There are parent letters to support each of the study skills habits represented in the letters STEP-UP. If you are teaching the program in a few lessons you can send home the STEP-UP to Better Grades Review Parent Letter after the last lesson.

Individual Students

- Once the students have learned the Core Lessons, you can focus on specific skills to support the academic needs of individual students.

- You can use the pre-test to identify areas needing improvement and then work together to set realistic academic goals.

- You can use the post-test to identify where improvements were made throughout the year and then celebrate their accomplishments.

{Session One}

STEP UP
to Better Grades

Overview: Developing strong study skills is the key to achieving academic success in school. It is these habits that will then carry on throughout a person's life into the world of post-secondary work. These lessons give an overview of the importance of instilling good study habits and how they connect schools with careers.

STEP-UP to Better Grades Contents:

STEP-UP to Better Grades Parent Letter
(Included on CD)

Core Lesson 1: STEP-UP Study Habits

Activity 1.1- STEP-UP Study Skills Pre-test

Activity 1.2- Good Study Habits

Activity 1.3- Molly and Tom's Career
(Good vs. Bad Study Habits)

Activity 1.4- Career Habits

CORE LESSON 1: STEP-UP Study Habits

OBJECTIVE: Students will gain an overview of good study habits and an introduction to STEP-UP to Better Grades.

MATERIALS: Dry Erase board and markers

PROCEDURES:

1. Ask students to raise their hand if they would like to get better grades in school. Draw STEPS on the board like Picture-A below and have the students guess what they see. Ask students what are STEPS used for. (They are used to get somewhere.) Sometimes they are short and sometimes they are long. Tell students that we are going to learn some study habits by going up the STEPS. Put the letters S-T-E-P-U-P on the stairs like Picture-B below. Tell the students that each letter represents a specific study skill or habit to help them succeed in school. Tell students by learning these "STEPS" or habits, you will STEP-UP to "BETTER GRADES."

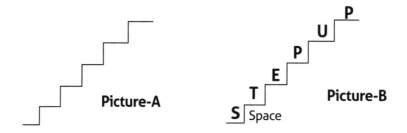

Picture-A   Picture-B

2. Ask students:
   - What is a habit? Something you do on a regular basis.
   - What is a good habit? Discuss answers. An example is brushing your teeth. Ask students why this is a good habit. Answers may be so you do not get cavities and it keeps your teeth clean and healthy.
   - What is a bad habit? Discuss answers. An example is picking your nose. Ask student why this is a bad habit. Answers may be it is unhygienic and it is unpleasant to witness.

3. Tell students that just like there are good and bad habits in life there are good and bad habits when it comes to studying. Ask students if the following are good or bad.
   - Taking your agenda home every day: GOOD
   - Not doing your homework: BAD
   - Studying for a test by using flash cards: GOOD
   - Watching TV while doing your homework: BAD

4. Let students know that it usually takes 21 days of repeatedly doing a task for it to become a habit so they will need to work at these habits to be successful. Tell students that it does not matter if they are good or bad in a subject; if they do these study habits, they will improve their grades.

SUMMARY: Ask students to state one thing they learned that will help them to STEP-UP to Better Grades.

ACTIVITY 1.1: STEP-UP Study Skills Pre-Test

OBJECTIVE: Students will identify their own study skills strengths and weaknesses.

MATERIALS: STEP-UP Study Skills Pre-test

Reproducible- STEP-UP Study Skills Goal Cards (one card per student)

Cards can be copied on card stock for durability

PROCEDURES:

1. Distribute STEP-UP Study Skills Pre-test to all students.

2. Tell students that they will read each statement and circle either

   5= Always, 4= Often, 3= Sometimes, 2= Rarely or

   1= Never for how that statement pertains to them.

3. Once students are finished, have them score their pre-test by adding up the numbers they circled.

4. Discuss pre-test statements and the scores. If they received a score of:

   • 30+   Excellent – Great study skills

   • 25-29   Good – Need help in a few areas

   • <24   Improvements needed- talk to your counselor or teacher for some assistance

5. Distribute STEP-UP Study Skills Goal Sheet to each student. Ask them to write down their two lowest numbers that they would like to make improvements on throughout the school year.

6. Have students tape their goal sheet in their agenda book or inside their desk by the front. Tell students as we go through these lessons to look for ways of reaching their goals.

7. Collect pre-tests for later lessons.

SUMMARY: Ask students to state one thing they learned that will help them to STEP-UP to Better Grades.

STEP-UP Study Skills Pre-test

Name: _____

DIRECTIONS: Please circle number that applies to you for each statement.

1 = Never   2 = Rarely   3 = Sometimes   4 = Often   5 = Always

1. I have a quiet place at home to do my work.   1   2   3   4   5

2. I bring all necessary materials to class;   1   2   3   4   5
paper and pencils.

3. I plan out all of my projects and assignments   1   2   3   4   5
so I am not rushed before they are due.

4. I PAY ATTENTION in class.   1   2   3   4   5

5. I follow directions in class the first time given.   1   2   3   4   5

6. I hand assignments in on time.   1   2   3   4   5

7. I study for my tests using different techniques.   1   2   3   4   5

Add the numbers from each statement to get a total score.   **Total Score** _____

Total score results:
30+   Excellent – Great study skills
25-29   Good – Need help in a few areas
< 24   Improvements needed – talk to teachers or your counselor or teacher for some assistance

STEP-UP Study Skills Goal Cards

My STEP-UP Study Skills Goals are:

1._____

2._____

My STEP-UP Study Skills Goals are:

1._____

2._____

My STEP-UP Study Skills Goals are:

1._____

2._____

My STEP-UP Study Skills Goals are:

1._____

2._____

My STEP-UP Study Skills Goals are:

1._____

2._____

My STEP-UP Study Skills Goals are:

1._____

2._____

My STEP-UP Study Skills Goals are:

1._____

2._____

My STEP-UP Study Skills Goals are:

1._____

2._____

ACTIVITY 1.2: Good Study Habits

OBJECTIVE: Students will be able to explore good study habits in school and at home.

MATERIALS: Reproducible - Good Study Habits (one for each group of 4-5 students)

PROCEDURES:

1. Divide class into groups of 4-5 students each.

2. Distribute Reproducible page – Good Study Habits for each group.

3. Have the group write as many good study habits that they can think of in three minutes.

4. Have each group share their list with the class. Discuss the importance of each good study habit.

5. Make sure you discuss some of the following study habits if they are not mentioned:

   - Quiet space to do homework
   - Have all the tools and supplies you need for assignments
   - Plan out your long-term projects
   - Pay attention to the teacher
   - Ask questions if you do not understand the material
   - Do your homework and turn it in to the teacher
   - Use an agenda to stay organized
   - Study for tests by reading and re-reading the material or using mnemonic devices

SUMMARY: Ask students to share one study habit that they would like to improve upon at school and/or at home.

DIRECTIONS: Write as many good study habits you can think of in 3 minutes on each race car.

ACTIVITY 1.3: Molly and Tom's Career

{Good vs. Bad Study Habits}

OBJECTIVE: Students will learn good vs. bad study habits and how they relate to the world of work.

MATERIALS: Reproducible story – Molly and Tom's Career

PROCEDURES:

1. Read the story of Molly and Tom's Career.

2. Discussion questions:

Who in the story had good study habits? (Tom)

Who had bad study habits? (Molly)

What were some of the poor study habits Molly had in the story?
- She lost her materials and those of co-workers.
- She missed deadlines.
- She rushed to complete her work.
- She had a messy work space.
- She didn't PAY ATTENTION to her supervisor's directions.

What were some of the good habits Tom had in the story?
- He did his best at all times.
- He used a calendar.
- He wrote down when tasks were due.
- He planned out his projects so he had enough time to finish them.
- He had an organized and clean work area.

- What kind of career do Molly and Tom have? They are students

- Who is their supervisor? Their teacher

- Discuss how many of the same study skills habits for school are the same as the habits in the working world.

{Good vs. Bad Study Habits} CONTINUED...

- What were some of the positive characteristics of Molly? She had great ideas and was very creative. Discuss how everyone has strengths and weaknesses, but sometimes we need to work on our weaknesses to be more successful.

- In the story, Molly and Tom have had to work together on various projects. How do you think Tom would feel if he was assigned to work with Molly by the teacher? He would feel frustrated because she is not very organized and does not meet deadlines. How would you feel if you were assigned to someone like Molly? Discuss the importance of having good study habits at all times so others would not feel frustrated when they are paired with you.

- The teacher has a very important task for a chosen student. Who do you think will get the opportunity to do it? Tom would most likely be chosen because of his good study habits. Discuss with the students that they may miss certain opportunities because of their poor study habits.

SUMMARY: Ask students to share one study habit that they would like to improve upon at school and/or at home.

Molly and Tom have worked together in the same place for many years. They arrive around 8:00am and work until 3:00pm, Monday through Friday. Both Molly and Tom have been assigned to the same area where they accomplish many of the same tasks. They even have had the chance to work together on various projects from time to time.

Molly, who has great ideas and is very creative, often forgets when deadlines are due. Her supervisor will expect the task on a certain day, but Molly is usually late with everything. Sometimes she doesn't even turn the task in, in hopes that her supervisor will forget. When her supervisor reminds her that she is past the deadline, she will often rush to finish it knowing that she could have done better.

Molly's working space is often messy and she always has a difficult time finding her materials. Co-workers will help her out, but she seems to lose their materials as well. When her supervisor gives Molly directions for a task, she often does the wrong job and has to re-do the task.

As for Tom, he realizes the importance of his job and makes sure that he gives his supervisor his best work at all times. He uses a calendar to write down when tasks are due from his supervisor and he gives himself plenty of time to complete them. Tom's working space is neat and orderly and he always knows where his materials are for when he needs them.

In two weeks, Molly and Tom's supervisor is going to select someone for a very important task. Both Molly and Tom would very much like to be chosen for that opportunity.

ACTIVITY 1.4: Career Habits

OBJECTIVE: Students will learn the necessary habits that are needed in various careers.

PROCEDURES:

1. Ask students: Why do you go to school? (To learn)
   How does school help you in the future? (To prepare us for a good job)

2. Ask students when they are no longer in school; what do they see themselves doing? (You may hear doctor, veterinarian, teacher, professional athlete, etc.) Pick a career that a student mentions and have the students describe the person in that career. What good habits or skills would this person need to have? For example, ask students what good habits or skills would a teacher need to have to be successful? Discuss answers.
   Here are some below:
   • Organized by having the necessary materials to teach that subject
   • Helpful by showing students what they don't understand
   • Dependable by coming to school on-time
   • Independent and Hard-working by being motivated to create lesson plans
   • Set goals to make sure the material is taught

3. Activity:
   • Have each student find a partner. Decide who will be person A and who will be person B.
   • Tell person B to go first by telling person A the habits and character traits needed for the career person B would choose.
   • After a few minutes, switch and have person A describe the habits and character traits needed for person A's chosen career.
   • Have a few students share the habits of their chosen career with the class.

4. Ask students to think of the habits that are the opposite of the ones they described. Use the example from above and have students give you the opposite habits and characteristics of a teacher.
   Here are some below:
   • Unorganized- Doesn't have the materials needed to teach that subject
   • Not helpful or patient when students do not understand something
   • Comes in late to school
   • Not prepared for the lessons

5. Ask students which teacher would they prefer to have and why.

6. Another example: Ask students if you were going to have surgery, would you want a doctor who read your chart, spoke with you about your injury, had all the necessary instruments ready, and knew the procedure very well or a doctor who didn't read your chart, was unorganized in the operating room, didn't have the tools needed, and arrived late to the operating room.

SUMMARY: Remind students that the skills they are learning now in school will be the skills they will need throughout their life.

SPACE

Having a Good Study Space

Overview: Students should make their SPACE at home, where they do their homework, as close to their SPACE at school. Student should:

- Do their homework at a table or desk
- Keep all toys and electronics away from the study SPACE
- Have a quiet study area
- Have TV, computers/other electronics turned off
- Work in a SPACE that has a lot of light

Ultimately, it should be free from distractions!

SPACE Contents:

SPACE Parent Letter (Included on CD)

Core Lesson 2• S-SPACE

Activity 2.1 • Do's and Don'ts

Activity 2.2 • Do's and Don'ts Home Survey

Activity 2.3 • Study SPACE

Activity 2.4 • Responsibility Scramble

Activity 2.5 • Responsibility Puzzle

Activity 2.6 • Mental Distractions

Activity 2.7 • Word Search Distractions

Activity 2.8 • Two Things at Once

Optional Activity 2.9 • *No Longer A Dilly Dally* Book

CORE LESSON 2: "S" - SPACE

OBJECTIVE: Students will learn the importance of keeping their homework space free from distractions.

MATERIALS: Dry Erase Board and Markers

PROCEDURES:

1. Review Core Lesson 1. Remind students that we will be learning six habits or skills that will help them to do better in school.

2. Draw six steps on the board.

3. Write the word SPACE next to the letter "S" on the board like the picture below.

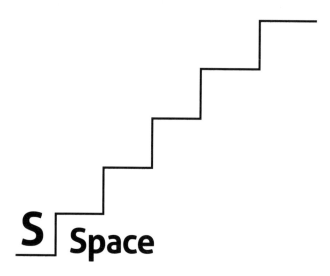

S | Space

4. Ask students what they think SPACE has to do with study habits? Explain that:
   • This is where you do your homework
   • Your homework space needs to be free from distractions

5. Ask students what gets in the way of doing their homework? Answers are: TV, electronic games, food, phone, friends, etc. Ask students what we call those things? Distractions.

6. Have students describe the classroom they are in right now. Ask them what do they see? Answers are: desks, chairs, text books, pencils, paper, overhead lights, etc.

CONTINUED...

7. Ask students the following questions:

- Is the TV playing your favorite show right now?
- Do we have video games here in the classroom?
- Is there a couch or bed in the classroom?
- Are there phones out on the desks?
- Do you see food on the desks?
  The answer is NO.

8. Tell students we want to make our SPACE at home, where we do our homework, to be as close to our SPACE at school- free from distractions. Your teacher does not have the TV playing so when you are studying at home you should have the TV off. You are sitting at a desk in school so you should not be sitting on the couch or bed to do your homework at home. And there is plenty of light in the classroom so you should do your homework with plenty of lights on in the room.

9. Ask student why they think this is important? Some answers are:

- It makes it easier to get homework done
- Helps students to stay focused

10. Ask students what can happen when you do your homework with the TV on? Some answers are:

- You will get distracted.
- Your homework will take longer to complete because you are watching the TV.
- You may make mistakes on your homework because you are distracted.

SUMMARY: Ask students what is the importance of SPACE when doing your homework? Keeping it free from distractions and making your SPACE at home, where you do your homework, look like your SPACE at school.

ACTIVITY 2.1: "Do's and Don'ts"

OBJECTIVE: Students will be able to identify a good study SPACE that is free from distractions.

MATERIALS: Do's and Don'ts Power Point or Reproducible Do's and Don'ts Picture Cards

PROCEDURES:

1. Do's and Don'ts Power Point
   - Put power point up on the screen.
   - Tell students that when a picture comes up they are to say either DO or DON'T. They will say DO if it is a good study SPACE habit or DON'T if it is a bad study SPACE habit or distraction.
   - Ask students why each one is a good study space habit or a bad study space habit.
   - Elaborate on certain slides. Comments are indicated in the notes section on the power point.

2. Do's and Don'ts Picture Cards
   - If you are using the picture cards, copy them on card stock ahead of time. Glue the comments for each picture on the back. It is best to laminate them so they will last longer.
   - Tell students that you are going to show them a picture card. When you show it they are to say either DO or DON'T. They will say DO if it is a good study SPACE habit or DON'T if it is a bad study SPACE habit or distraction.
   - Ask students why each one is a good study space habit or a bad study space habit.
   - Elaborate on certain picture cards.

SUMMARY: Ask students what they learned about having a good study SPACE.

VARIATION: Write the words "Do and Don't" on the board. Under each word have students name the good SPACE habits and the bad SPACE habits to make a list.

Do's and Don'ts Picture Cards

| **DO!** You always want plenty of light when doing your homework. | **DON'T!** Have a snack first and then do your homework. You don't want your homework to get all greasy too. |

| **DO!** You want to sit in a chair and at a table when doing your homework. | **DON'T!** Keep your SPACE free from toys and distractions. |

Do's and Don'ts Picture Cards

DO! You always want a quiet place to study.

DON'T! You want to keep your study SPACE free from toys and distractions. You can play with them after you finish your homework.

DO! Using the kitchen table to do your home work may be the closest SPACE to your desk at school.

DON'T! Texting and talking to your friends can distract you from your homework.

Do's and Don'ts Picture Cards

DON'T! Do not study in an area that is really noisy.	**DO!** Always use a desk or table when doing your homework.

DON'T! It's not a good idea to do your homework while in bed.	**DO!** You always want enough light when doing your homework.

Do's and Don'ts Picture Cards

DON'T! Play your video games as a reward for completing your homework.

DO! Sit at a desk to do your homework if you can.

DON'T! You don't have candy out during school while you are doing your work so have a treat after you finish your homework. You might get your homework sticky too.

DON'T! Be careful with drinks at your table or desk while doing your homework, you may spill them. I also talk with them about healthy snack and drink choices.

Do's and Don'ts Picture Cards

DO! It is important to sit up straight while doing your homework.	**DON'T!** Keep your SPACE free from toys and distractions.

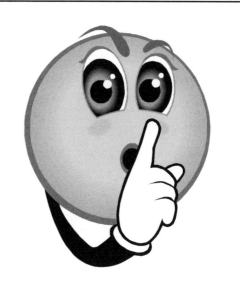

DON'T! Do not do your homework on the couch. It is hard to write with books on your lap. Remind the students that if they are reading a book, it is fine to sit on the couch. This habit has to do with written work.	**DO!** Keep your SPACE as quiet as possible.

Do's and Don'ts Picture Cards

DON'T! The TV will distract you while you are doing your homework.	**DON'T!** Keep your SPACE free from distractions.

MAYBE! Some students can study while listening to music. If you find that you are getting distracted by the music, then you need to turn it off.	**DON'T!** Eat a snack before or after you do your homework.

Do's and Don'ts Picture Cards

DO! Focus on your homework. Keep distractions away.

DO! A coffee table at home may be the closest SPACE for doing homework.

DON'T! You will have a hard time concentrating if you are too comfortable.

DO! Making your SPACE at home like your SPACE at school.

ACTIVITY 2.2: Do's and Don'ts Home Survey

OBJECTIVE: Students will identify areas for improvement for eliminating distractions in their Study SPACE for doing homework.

MATERIALS: Reproducible- Do's and Don'ts Home Survey (one for each student)
Pencils

PROCEDURES:

1. Distribute Do's and Don'ts Home Survey to each student.

2. Have students take the survey independently.

3. Ask students the following questions:
   • What could students do at home if they circled "I DON'T" for using a table or desk to change that?

   • What could students do at home if they circled "I DON'T" for having a clean area to work in at home?

   • What could students do at home if they circled "I DON'T" for having a quiet area to study in at home?

   • What could students do at home if they circled "I DON'T" for having a well-lit area to study in at home?

4. Ask students who would like to share with the group an area that they would like to work on improving at home.

SUMMARY: Encourage students to create a positive study SPACE at home.

Home SPACE Do's and Don'ts

Name: _____

DIRECTIONS: Please circle either "I do" or "I don't" after each question.

1. I use a table or desk to do my homework?   **I DO**   **I DON'T**

2. I study in a clean area? (No food, toys, etc)   **I DO**   **I DON'T**

3. I study in a quiet area? (No TV, siblings, etc.)   **I DO**   **I DON'T**

4. I study in a well-lit area?   **I DO**   **I DON'T**

If you circled an "I don't," what could you do to change it to an "I do?" _____

_____

_____

_____

_____

Are you willing to try it?   YES   NO

Having a quiet, clean, and well-lit place to do your homework is important. Please discuss this with your parent.

ACTIVITY 2.3: My Study SPACE

OBJECTIVE: Students will learn how to visualize a clear image of what a good study SPACE looks like.

MATERIALS: Reproducible- Study SPACE (one for each student)
Crayons, markers, or colored pencils

PROCEDURES:

1. Distribute Study SPACE worksheet to each student.

2. Have students circle everything they need in their study SPACE.

3. Have students place an "X" on those items that would not be good to have in their study SPACE.

4. Have students discuss why they put an "X" or a circle on the items.

5. Have students discuss any changes they need to make so their study SPACE is more effective.

SUMMARY: Ask students why it is important to have a positive study SPACE at home.

My Study SPACE

DIRECTIONS: Circle everything you need in your study SPACE and "X" out those items that would not be good to have in your study SPACE.

ACTIVITY 2.4: Responsibility Scramble

OBJECTIVE: Students will work together to spell out the word *Responsibility.*

MATERIALS: Reproducible- Responsibility Scramble (one set for each group of 4-5 students)

PROCEDURES:

1. Preparation work:
   - Copy the Responsibility Scramble sheet onto cardstock as many times as you need so each group has a set.
   - Laminate it to make it stronger.
   - Cut out each letter.
   - Put each set in a baggie or clip together.

2. Divide the class into groups of four or five students.

3. Tell students that you are going to give them a baggie full of letters. They are to rearrange all the letters to make one word.
   (Optional: You can give a prize to the group that puts the word together first).

4. Once all the groups have put the letters together to make the word *Responsibility*, ask the following questions:
   - What does the word *Responsibility* mean?
   - What does responsibility have to do with your study SPACE at home?
   - Whose responsibility is it to make sure you have a good study SPACE at home that is free from distractions?
   - How can you take responsibility for your study SPACE at home?
   - What are some other areas in your life that you need to take responsibility?

SUMMARY: Encourage students to take responsibility with homework without being told.

Responsibility Scramble

R E S
P O N
S I B
I L I
T Y

ACTIVITY 2.5: Responsibility Puzzle

OBJECTIVE: Students will work together in teams to put the *Responsibility* puzzle together.

MATERIALS: Reproducible- Responsibility Puzzle (one puzzle cut apart for each group of 4-5 students) Optional: Purchase ready-made blank puzzles. Write the word *responsibility* on it and then put the pieces in a baggie for each group.

PROCEDURES:

1. Divide the class into groups of four or five students.

2. Tell students that you are going to give them a baggie full of puzzle pieces. They are to put the pieces together to find the key word (Optional: You can give a prize to the group that puts the puzzle together first).

3. Once all the groups have put their puzzles together to make the word *Responsibility*, ask the following questions:
   • What does the word *Responsibility* mean?
   • What does responsibility have to do with your study SPACE at home?
   • Whose responsibility is it to make sure you have a good study SPACE at home that is free from distractions?
   • How can you take responsibility for your study SPACE at home?
   • What are some other areas in your life that you need to take responsibility?

SUMMARY: Encourage students to take responsibility with homework without being told.

ACTIVITY 2.6: Mental Distractions

OBJECTIVE: Students will learn various positive thinking strategies for overcoming mental distractions.

MATERIALS: Reproducible- Mental Distractions (cards copied on cardstock and cut apart)

PROCEDURES:

1. Ask students what they think mental distractions are? Discuss that sometimes when students do their homework they have a difficult time concentrating because they are thinking about something else. Just like toys or electronics can be a distraction, thoughts about our school work or what we would rather be doing can distract us from doing our homework.

2. Ask students to name some mental distractions they have when doing their homework. Some answers are:
   • I wonder what my friends are doing   • I really want to play my video game   • This work is hard

3. Have a student come to the front to pick a card and read the mental distraction. Have that student give a suggestion for how to overcome the mental distraction.

4. Ask students if they have ever thought this while doing their homework and what they have done to overcome the mental distraction. Discuss strategies.

5. Repeat with the other mental distraction cards.
   Possible positive thinking strategies:
   • Tell yourself that after you finish this subject, you can take a break and spend 30 minutes doing what you want.
   • Tell yourself, "I know this is hard, but I can do it."
   • Tell yourself that the longer you think about other things, the longer your homework will take and you won't get to do what you want.
   • Take five minutes to stand up and do 10 jumping jacks. Sometimes taking a few minutes to do something else can help you focus.
   • Use a timer and tell yourself that you can take a break in 30 minutes.
   • Tell yourself that you will feel good when you have completed all your homework.
   • Finish your hardest subject first and then the easy one will be more fun.

SUMMARY: Ask students to share which positive thinking strategy would work best for them.

VARIATIONS: Divide the class into groups and have them brainstorm a list of positive thinking strategies to share with the class.

Mental Distractions

I really want to read that good book I have been reading.	I want to go and play outside.
I am failing this subject so why should I try?	My friend asked me to call after school.
I almost beat my highest video game score.	This homework is too hard. I give up!
I can do my homework later.	My favorite TV show is on right now.
I am so tired.	I'll just do this in study hall tomorrow.

ACTIVITY 2.7: Word Search Distractions

OBJECTIVE: Students will experience working on assignments with and without distractions.

MATERIALS: Reproducible – Word Search Distractions A and B copied on one sheet front and back (one for each student), TV or Video, Music Player, Musical Instrument

PROCEDURES:

1. Ask students to name the noise distractions they may experience at home. Some answers are: TV, Radio, Dog, Siblings yelling, etc.

2. Turn on the TV to an appropriate show or play a video. Ask students if this would distract them at home.

3. Play some music in addition to the TV being on in the room. Ask students if this would distract them to have two things playing.

4. Start playing a musical instrument such as a recorder or tambourine. Ask students if they would have trouble concentrating now that there are three things playing.

5. Mute music and TV. Distribute Reproducible Word Search Distractions to students and have them turn it to side A. Once all students have their papers tell them that they will have two minutes to find as many words as they can. Continue playing all three noises- the TV, Music, and the Instrument while they are working. You can even start talking to some of the students.

6. Say "stop" when time is up. Ask students:
   - How many words did you find?
   - How many of you had a hard time concentrating?
   - Did anyone start watching the TV?
   - Did you find yourself looking up and around more?

7. Now turn everything off so the room is quiet. Tell students to turn their paper over to Word Search Distractions B. Tell them that once again they will have two minutes to find as many words as they can.

8. Say "stop" when time is up. Ask students:
   - How many words did you find?
   - Were you able to concentrate more this time?
   - How did it feel when it was quiet as opposed to when it was noisy?

SUMMARY: Remind students when they are doing their homework that they will get more done when their SPACE is free from distractions.

Word Search Distractions [A]

DIRECTIONS: Find as many words in two minutes.

```
J  B  Y  G  B  E  P  H  O  N  E  X  N  U  Z
S  I  P  E  X  O  A  N  A  W  P  D  O  M  W
L  C  O  M  P  U  T  E  R  R  C  N  I  D  Z
E  H  R  T  W  U  V  X  J  D  A  P  T  V  G
E  M  N  W  T  F  O  N  Q  U  F  A  C  I  G
P  T  E  L  E  V  I  S  I  O  N  R  A  K  F
Y  K  F  Y  R  H  Z  G  F  H  K  E  R  R  R
T  E  I  U  Q  D  D  H  Q  C  J  T  T  O  I
V  H  B  X  I  R  P  P  V  Z  W  S  S  W  E
I  S  G  H  B  H  C  U  O  C  P  I  I  E  N
D  S  Q  I  Z  J  R  F  Z  Z  F  S  D  M  D
E  M  H  B  L  F  O  U  B  V  O  M  K  O  S
O  I  K  R  M  F  O  O  D  P  L  R  K  H  J
B  G  A  J  B  X  B  S  C  C  F  D  I  S  C
U  C  A  K  O  Q  U  W  K  S  E  D  E  X  Y
```

Computer	Friends	Sister
Couch	Homework	Sleepy
Desk	Light	Television
Distraction	Phone	Video
Food	Quiet	

Word Search Distractions [B]

DIRECTIONS: Find as many words in two minutes.

```
G  I  C  R  E  H  T  O  R  B  N  J  M  Z  A
E  T  L  K  R  Q  M  F  W  B  S  O  S  S  V
U  P  S  P  E  L  G  P  O  C  C  M  I  C  C
Y  I  G  J  S  F  D  O  C  Y  I  J  R  S  P
D  O  I  G  P  P  K  O  N  G  N  S  J  L  E
U  M  K  N  O  S  B  W  N  V  O  N  U  H  U
T  Y  R  O  N  R  A  I  H  C  R  A  G  C  E
S  X  A  O  S  D  W  D  N  K  T  C  W  Y  L
E  W  D  I  I  L  K  W  E  D  C  K  J  U  B
W  M  I  G  B  Y  U  M  R  P  E  S  B  M  A
I  K  O  Y  I  F  A  I  V  Y  L  Y  C  F  T
Q  Z  N  W  L  G  N  C  E  N  E  I  B  P  R
T  S  O  S  I  K  H  D  Q  L  H  T  O  Y  S
X  F  H  Y  T  Y  Z  S  I  I  U  O  J  X  J
D  G  T  T  Y  Q  E  C  A  P  S  W  H  U  L
```

Books	Game	Space
Brother	Noise	Study
Chair	Radio	Table
Drink	Responsibility	Toys
Electronics	Snacks	

ACTIVITY 2.8: Two Things at Once

OBJECTIVE: Students will learn how distractions can affect their learning.

MATERIALS: Two Things at Once sheet (one for each student)
Pencils

PROCEDURES:

1. Ask students what happens when they try and do two things at once. Discuss answers. Often one or both of the activities suffer because their attention is divided between the two tasks.

2. Distribute the Two Things at Once sheet to students upside down. Tell the students that when you say go, they are to turn their paper over and write down as many animals that they can think of in about two minutes. (Optional) You can tell them that you will give a prize to the student who gets the most.

3. While they are writing down the animals, start reading *The Football Game* story out loud.

{The Football Game Story}

It is the night of the long awaited state championship game for two rival high school football teams. The 12 and 2 Duluth Lions are playing the 13 and 1 Jesup Eagles on this beautiful fall night at the Georgia University Stadium. The star Duluth Lions quarterback, Tommy Harper, is returning after a torn hamstring in his left leg. Fans are so excited he is back, they feel the Lions will certainly clinch the title. As for the Jesup Eagles, recruiters have been following their star running back for weeks now. Everyone is anxiously awaiting which college Patrick Mann is going to choose.

It is now 7:30pm and kickoff is about to begin. The Lions win the coin toss and choose to receive. Both coaches are running up and down the field yelling as the players take their positions. The whistle blows and there's the kick...Chris Green makes the catch. He runs 20 yards, now 50, now 80 total yards for a touchdown! Amazing!! The Lions are surely on their way to a great game!

4. When you finish the story, have the students answer the questions at the bottom of their paper about the story. Read the answers and have them check off which ones they got correct. Ask them how they did. Discuss how difficult it is to do two things at once.

CONTINUED....

Answers to the Football Game Story

1. What two teams played in the championship game? (The Duluth Lions and the Jesup Eagles)

2. What was the weather like for the game? (Beautiful fall night)

3. What was the name of the quarterback who tore a hamstring? (Tommy Harper)

4. What position does Patrick Mann play? (Running Back)

5. What time was kickoff? (7:30pm)

6. Who won the coin toss? (The Lions)

7. How many total yards did Chris Green run for a touchdown? (80 yards)

5. Ask students what happens at home or at school when they try to do two things at once.

SUMMARY: Remind the students that it is important to keep their SPACE free from distractions while doing their homework. Tell the students that it is difficult to do two things at the same time and do well on both.

Two Things at Once

Name: _____

DIRECTIONS: Write down as many animals that you can think of in two minutes.

1. _____
2. _____
3. _____
4. _____
5. _____
6. _____
7. _____
8. _____
9. _____
10. _____

11. _____
12. _____
13. _____
14. _____
15. _____
16. _____
17. _____
18. _____
19. _____
20. _____

{The Football Game Story}

1. What two teams played in the championship game? _____
2. What was the weather like for the game? _____
3. What was the name of the quarterback who tore a hamstring? _____
4. What position does Patrick Mann play? _____
5. What time was kickoff? _____
6. Who won the coin toss? _____
7. How many total yards did Chris Green run for a touchdown? _____

OPTIONAL ACTIVITY 2.9: No Longer A Dilly Dally

OBJECTIVE: Students will learn the importance of being responsible and using time wisely.

MATERIALS: Book – *No Longer A Dilly Dally* by Carl Sommer
Advance Publishing, Inc.
ISBN 1-57537-001-8
Can be found on Amazon or at any major book store
Reproducible – No Longer A Dilly Dally Survey

PROCEDURES:

1. Ask students what the word Procrastination means. It means to delay or put off something until a later time or date.

2. Ask students the following:
   • How do students procrastinate? (Play video games, watch TV, listen to music, talk to a friend, etc.)
   • Why do students procrastinate with their school work? (They don't want to do their homework or that task. They see other things, such as video games and the TV as something they would rather do. They may see their homework as too hard.)
   • What happens when they procrastinate? (They don't get their homework completed. They may get a lower grade. There may be a consequence)
   • What are some excuses students might give for procrastinating?
     (I don't get it; I'll never get this right; I can do it later; I'll ask my teacher tomorrow)

3. Read the book *No Longer A Dilly Dally* by Carl Sommer

4. Discussions Questions:
   • Where did Family Work Play decide to live? (They looked for a place where they could find a lot of food)
   • Where did Family Dilly Dally decide to live? (They looked for a place where they could have a lot of fun)
   • What did Papa Work Play say about work and play? (They work first and play later)
   • Did Family Work Play procrastinate? (No) What was their plan for the day? (They dug their basement and gathered food during the day then relaxed in the evening.)
   • What did Family Dilly Dally say about work and play? (They just wanted to have fun.)

OPTIONAL ACTIVITY 2.9: No Longer A Dilly Dally

CONTINUED....

- What was Family Dilly Dally's plan for the day? (They slept late, relaxed during the day, and then looked for food in the evening) Did they procrastinate? (Yes)

- What was Family Work Play's house like by the end of the summer? (They had a nice house and a basement full of food for the winter.)

- What happened to Family Dilly Dally because they procrastinated during the summer? (They had a small house far away from food and nothing in their basement for the winter)

- What happened to Family Dilly Dally during the winter? (They had to look for food every day in the snow)

- What did Family Work Play do during the winter? (They relaxed and played)

- What did papa Dilly Dally say to his family at the end of the winter? (We are now going to be called Family Work First)

- Why did papa Dilly Dally change their name? (Because they learned that it is important to be responsible and work first, then play. They also learned not to procrastinate.)

5. Distribute Reproducible – No Longer A Dilly Dally Survey to each student.

6. Have students take the survey according to the directions.

7. When they have finished, have them add up the numbers to get a total score. Have students look at the key based on the number they added up.

8. Read and discuss each survey statement. Ask students why each of these is important to being a successful student.

9. Have students circle the two statements that they scored the highest on in the survey. Ask the students what they do to keep that score high.

10. Have students cross out the two statements that they scored the lowest on in the survey. Go over each statement and discuss what they could do to improve in that area.

11. Have students write down one suggestion, for each low scored statement, for how to improve in that area.

12. Ask students what they can do or say to themselves to not procrastinate. Discuss answers.

SUMMARY: Remind students how good it feels when they work first and play later.

No Longer A Dilly Dally Survey

DIRECTIONS: Complete the survey by circling the appropriate number that is indicated. Add up your points to see how you scored at the bottom.

		Always	Often	Sometimes	Rarely	Never
1.	I start my homework right away after school or at the designated time.	5	4	3	2	1
2.	I turn my homework in on time.	5	4	3	2	1
3.	I keep my study space free from distractions.	5	4	3	2	1
4.	I use my time wisely during school.	5	4	3	2	1
5.	I use my time wisely at home.	5	4	3	2	1
6.	I stay organized with my school work so I do not procrastinate.	5	4	3	2	1
7.	I plan out projects instead of waiting until the last minute.	5	4	3	2	1
8.	I study for tests a little bit each night before the test.	5	4	3	2	1
9.	I am responsible.	5	4	3	2	1
10.	I work first and then play later.	5	4	3	2	1
Total:						

46+   Excellent! You really use your time wisely.

40-45   Good job! You use your time pretty well.

34-39   Okay! You need some help in a few areas.

25-33   Looks like there are several areas that need improvement.

10-29   Let's talk!

My Score is: _____

1. Circle the two areas above where you scored the highest. Great job!

2. X-Out the two areas that need the most improvement.

3. What can you do to make improvements on the ones you crossed out? _____

_____

Tools
Staying Organized

Overview: Just like doctors, plumbers, computer programmers and other various professions have their own tools to do their job, it is important for students to have their own Study Tools to be successful as well. Making sure students use some kind of agenda or calendar helps them know what is due. And having a folder to keep all their assignments in keeps their papers neat and organized. Many students work hard on their assignments, but only to lose them inside a messy desk. By using the Tools to stay organized, students will feel more effective in school.

TOOLS Contents:

TOOLS Parent Letter (Included on CD)

Core Lesson 3 • T- TOOLS

Activity 3.1 • My Study Toolbox

Activity 3.2 • What Happened to My Grades?

Activity 3.3 • The Two Book bags Game

Activity 3.4 • Look at My Desk!

Activity 3.5 • Who is Checking My Desk?

Activity 3.6 • What's My Schedule?

Activity 3.7 • Career Tools Game

Activity 3.8 • Tools Survey

Activity 3.9 • Name That Tool Crossword

CORE LESSON 3: "T" - TOOLS

OBJECTIVE: Students will learn the important tools of a student.

MATERIALS: Agenda Book or Weekly Agenda Sheet.
(Note: Some schools provide Agenda Books for their students. If not, copy the Weekly Agenda so each student has four copies: one for each week. Make more copies for the next month).

Homework Folder (Note: Some schools provide these already pre-printed for their students. If not, have students purchase a pocket folder before the lesson or if your budget allows, purchase them for the students).

Permanent Marker (only needed if folders are not pre-printed)

PROCEDURES:

1. Draw the steps on the board like picture A below. Put the letter "S" and the word SPACE on the first step like in picture B. Review by asking students what they remember about the letter "S" for SPACE. (It is to keep their study SPACE at home free from distractions).

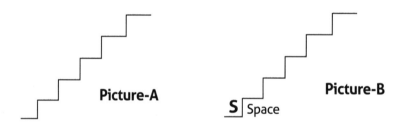

Picture-A   Picture-B

2. Tell students that the next letter we are going to talk about in STEP-UP is "T." Put the letter "T" and the word TOOLS on the second step like picture C below.

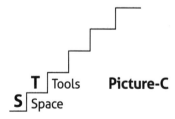

Picture-C

3. Ask students:
   • What are the tools of a doctor?
   • What are the tools of a construction worker?
   • What are the tools of a chef?

4. Ask students what are the tools of a student? They will name pencils, pens, markers, books, paper, book bag, etc. If they have not mentioned "Agenda Book" and "Homework Folder," say that you have not heard the TWO most important tools of a student. Allow students to continue guessing. Once the students have guessed them or you have told them, discuss the importance of each one.

CORE LESSON 3: "T" - TOOLS

CONTINUED...

5. Show students an Agenda Book and tell them that it is the most important tool of a student. Ask students to tell you why the Agenda Book is important. Tell students that they can get home and have all their books and supplies, but if they do not have their Agenda Book they will not know what they need to do.

6. If students already have an agenda book, have them take it out. If not, distribute the Weekly Agenda copies to each student.

7. Open the Agenda Book and discuss how to use it. Show students where to write down the assignment for each subject that a teacher says or writes on the board. (Some pre-printed agendas already have the dates for the year printed at the top. If you are using the Reproducible- Weekly Agenda, have the students write the date on the line next to the day. You can also make several copies to staple together to make one or two months).

8. Put the acronym - AGENDA lengthwise on the board. Discuss each letter to help them remember the importance of using their agenda.

A - Assignments (Write down assignments by subject in the agenda daily)

G - Goals (Prioritize each assignment. Check off when completed)

E - Everyday (Write in the agenda, look at the agenda, and take the agenda home every day.)

N - Notes (Write down notes or reminders such as field trip money, project supplies, etc.)

D - Due Dates (Write down test dates and project due dates)

A - Ask (Ask for help or clarification on assignments or due dates)

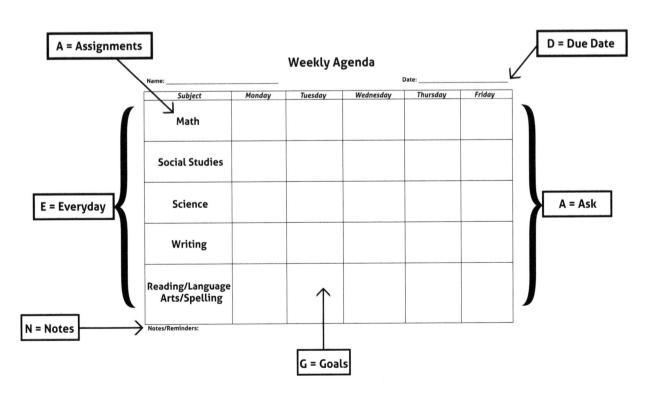

CONTINUED...

9. By remembering the letters AGENDA, ask students how the agenda helps them? (To stay organized)

10. Ask students why the Homework Folder is an important tool of a student. Some answers are: This is where students can keep their assignments neat. It also keeps the assignments from getting lost.

11. Show students a folder with the words Homework Folder written on the front cover and the words "To Do" on the inside pocket of one side and "To Turn In" on the other side. Tell students that when they are at home and they finish their assignment, they should put it in their Homework Folder on the side that says, "To Turn in." Also, when they are at school and they have an assignment to finish, they should put it in their Homework Folder on the side that says "To Do" at home.

12. Have students take out their Homework Folder or pocket folder. The Homework Folder may already have the words "Homework Folder" on the cover and "To Do" and "To Turn In" on the inside pockets. If not, have students use a permanent marker to write them on the folder.

SUMMARY: Ask students: What are the two most important tools of a student? Tell students that you will be checking to see if they are using these tools on a daily basis.

Weekly Agenda

Name: _____   Date: _____

Subject	Monday	Tuesday	Wednesday	Thursday	Friday
Math					
Social Studies					
Science					
Writing					
Reading/Language Arts/Spelling					

Notes/Reminders: _____

_____

ACTIVITY 3.1: My Study Toolbox

OBJECTIVE: Students will learn the importance of having a study toolbox nearby while studying.

MATERIALS: Toolbox- Made ahead of time with school supplies in it.
A plastic shoebox works great or even a cardboard shoebox. (Optional: Decorate the box)
Reproducible- My Study Toolbox
Reproducible- My Study Toolbox List (Variation)

PROCEDURES:

1. Ask students to raise their hand if they ever had to get up from doing their homework because their pencil broke. Or they needed glue or markers for an assignment.

2. Tell students to watch you as you act out what this might look like at home.
   - Pretend that you are at home doing your homework and your pencil broke.
   - Get up and start walking to another place in the room to get a pencil.
   - Tell the students that to get to where the pencils are you have to go past the family room where your little brother is watching TV and it happens to be one of your favorite shows. As you start walking through the family room you see your favorite show on and you stop. Make a look like you are staring at the TV with your mouth open. Don't move, just keep on staring. At this time the students will start laughing.
   - Break character and ask students whose voice would you usually hear at this time. (Parent's voice). And what would they say? "Why aren't you doing your homework?" And your response would be? I just had to get up to get a pencil. But now 30 minutes have gone by because you went to get a pencil.

3. Show students a Study Toolbox. Open it up and pull out all the school supplies that fit in it.

4. Tell students that they need to keep a Study Toolbox nearby when doing homework so if they need something it will be right there. Ask students why they think this is important? It is so they do not have to get up to get something. When they get up, they can get distracted just like in the scene they just saw. And they may also have a hard time getting back in the groove of studying.

5. Distribute Reproducible- My Study Toolbox to all students. Have them draw all the items they can think of that would go in their Toolbox.

ACTIVITY 3.1: My Study Toolbox

CONTINUED...

6. Have students share all the items they came up with. Students can add items mentioned that they did not include on their picture as students share. Read off the following as examples of Toolbox items if they are not mentioned:

- Pencils
- Erasers
- Glue Sticks
- Ruler
- Pencil Sharpener

- Tape
- Colored pencils
- Crayons
- Pens
- Sticky Notes

- Scissors
- Markers
- Liquid Glue
- Highlighters
- Index Cards

7. Have students take home their Toolbox picture. Have them ask their parents/guardians to help them put together a shoebox full of these items. Optional: Ask local organizations to put together these boxes at the beginning of the year for needy families.

SUMMARY: Ask students: Why is it important to have a toolbox nearby when studying? So you have what you need and you don't have to get up.

VARIATION: If budget permits, purchase plastic tubs for the students to decorate and fill them with some of the Toolbox items. Send home Reproducible- My Study Toolbox List of items for parents/guardians to complete at home.

My Study Toolbox

DIRECTIONS: Draw various school supplies inside the Toolbox.

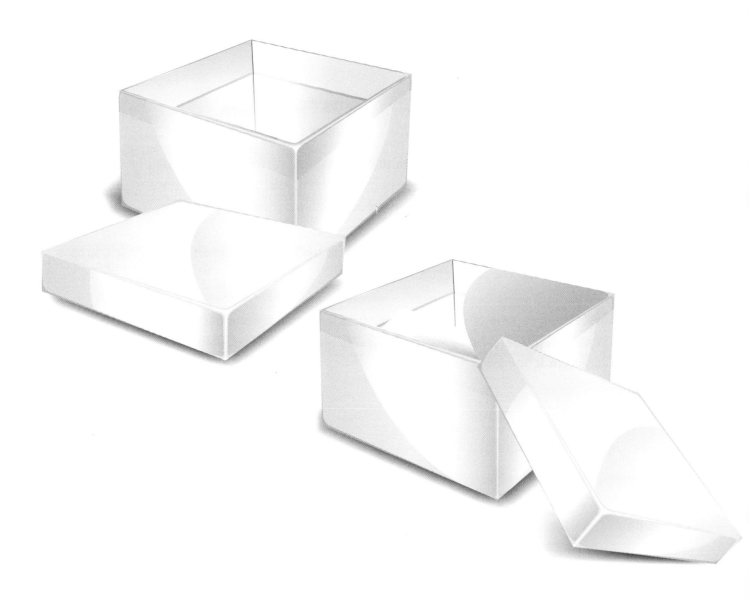

My Study Toolbox List

Dear Parent/Guardian,

Please help your child make a Study Toolbox to keep at home. This should be brought out every time your child does homework. Often children will get distracted when they have to get up to find something while doing homework so having their own Study Toolbox will keep their supplies nearby. Below is a possible list of items to include:
Thank you!

SOME ITEMS TO PUT IN MY STUDY TOOLBOX

- Pencils
- Erasers
- Markers
- Crayons
- Highlighters
- Tape
- Colored pencils
- Glue Sticks
- Liquid Glue
- Pencil sharpener
- Scissors
- Sticky Notes
- Index Cards
- Pens
- Ruler

My Study Toolbox List

Dear Parent/Guardian,

Please help your child make a Study Toolbox to keep at home. This should be brought out every time your child does homework. Often children will get distracted when they have to get up to find something while doing homework so having their own Study Toolbox will keep their supplies nearby. Below is a possible list of items to include:
Thank you!

SOME ITEMS TO PUT IN MY STUDY TOOLBOX

- Pencils
- Erasers
- Markers
- Crayons
- Highlighters
- Tape
- Colored pencils
- Glue Sticks
- Liquid Glue
- Pencil sharpener
- Scissors
- Sticky Notes
- Index Cards
- Pens
- Ruler

ACTIVITY 3.2: "What happened to my grades?"

OBJECTIVE: Students will learn how their grades are affected by low test scores.

MATERIALS: Reproducible- "What happened to my grades? – A (For younger grades) or Reproducible- "What happened to my grades? – B (For older grades)

PROCEDURES:

1. Ask students:
   - Have you ever thought you were doing well in a subject, but then were disappointed when you received a low test grade?
   - What happened to your grade in that subject?

2. Distribute Reproducible- "What happened to my grades?" (either A or B)

3. Have students complete Problem 1 by filling in the blanks. Tell students, for example, on their first science test they received an 87. On their second science test they received a 96. But on their third science test they received a 30. When added together and divided by three they got an average of 71. Ask students what happened on the third test. Discuss answers. Tell students that you may have forgotten to use your agenda and didn't know when the test was so you were not prepared. The low grade of 30 pulled their grade down to a D where they received a high A and B on the other tests. Tell students that this is how every test score affects your grade point average.

4. Tell students that this is why using our tools is important in school. By using the agenda and making it a habit, students will always be prepared for tests.

5. Have students complete Problem 2 by filling in the blanks. Discuss what happened to the grade when the test score of 30 was replaced by an 80. It went up. They now have an average of 88 or high B. Ask students which one they would prefer, the grade from Problem 1 or Problem 2. Ask students why they think the grade went up. It was because they studied for the test.

6. Continue with Problems 3 and 4. Ask students if they would rather have a grade of A with a 90 average in Problem 4 or a C with an average of 75 in Problem 3. Finish Problems 5 and 6 and discuss the difference between the two. Show students how just one test can make a difference between receiving an A or a C.

7. If you are using "What happened to my grades?- B, have students try and solve the bonus question. If they are stuck, tell them that they know there are four test scores so the number four will go in the second blank. They can then multiply 83 x 4= 332. Add up the other test scores to get 240. Subtract 240 from 332 to get the answer 92.

Note: You can also have the students do this activity in groups to save on computing time by assigning each group a problem.

SUMMARY: Remind students that every test is important because it makes a difference to your grade point average.

Name: _____

DIRECTIONS: Add the following numbers and then divide by the number of scores listed to get the average.

1. $\begin{array}{r} 87 \\ 96 \\ +\ 30 \\ \hline \end{array}$ ___ ÷ ___ = <u>71</u>	**2.** $\begin{array}{r} 87 \\ 96 \\ +\ 80 \\ \hline \end{array}$ ___ ÷ ___ = <u>88</u>
3. $\begin{array}{r} 84 \\ 20 \\ 96 \\ +\ 100 \\ \hline \end{array}$ ___ ÷ ___ = <u>75</u>	**4.** $\begin{array}{r} 84 \\ 80 \\ 96 \\ +\ 100 \\ \hline \end{array}$ ___ ÷ ___ = <u>90</u>
5. $\begin{array}{r} 90 \\ 0 \\ 95 \\ 95 \\ +\ 100 \\ \hline \end{array}$ ___ ÷ ___ = <u>76</u>	**6.** $\begin{array}{r} 90 \\ 80 \\ 95 \\ 95 \\ +\ 100 \\ \hline \end{array}$ ___ ÷ ___ = <u>92</u>

90-100	=	A
80-89	=	B
74-79	=	C
70-73	=	D

69 and below is failing

"What happened to my grades?"-B

Name: _____

DIRECTIONS: Add the following numbers and then divide by the number of scores listed to get the average.

1.   87
         96
  + 30
     ——
 	
    ÷   =
___   ___   ___
	2. 87
	         96
	  + 80
	     ——
	
	    ÷ =
	___ ___ ___

3.   84
         20
         96
 + 100
     ——
 	
    ÷   =
___   ___   ___
	4. 84
	         80
	         96
	 + 100
	     ——
	
	    ÷ =
	___ ___ ___

5.   90
          0
         95
         95
 + 100
     ——
 	
    ÷   =
___   ___   ___
	6. 90
	         80
	         95
	         95
	 + 100
	     ——
	
	    ÷ =
	___ ___ ___

7.   78
            87
            75
        + ?

    ___ ÷ ___ = <u> 83 </u>

Bonus

90-100	=	A
80-89	=	B
74-79	=	C
70-73	=	D
69 and below is failing		

TEACHER KEY

1. $\quad\quad$ 87 $\quad\quad$ 96 $\quad +$ 30 $\quad\quad\rule{2cm}{0.4pt}$ $\quad$ 213 $\div$ 3 $=$ 71	**2.** $\quad\quad$ 87 $\quad\quad$ 96 $\quad +$ 80 $\quad\quad\rule{2cm}{0.4pt}$ $\quad$ 263 $\div$ 3 $=$ 88
3. $\quad\quad$ 84 $\quad\quad$ 20 $\quad\quad$ 96 $\quad +$ 100 $\quad\quad\rule{2cm}{0.4pt}$ $\quad$ 300 $\div$ 4 $=$ 75	**4.** $\quad\quad$ 84 $\quad\quad$ 80 $\quad\quad$ 96 $\quad +$ 100 $\quad\quad\rule{2cm}{0.4pt}$ $\quad$ 360 $\div$ 4 $=$ 90
5. $\quad\quad$ 90 $\quad\quad$ 0 $\quad\quad$ 95 $\quad\quad$ 95 $\quad +$ 100 $\quad\quad\rule{2cm}{0.4pt}$ $\quad$ 380 $\div$ 5 $=$ 76	**6.** $\quad\quad$ 90 $\quad\quad$ 80 $\quad\quad$ 95 $\quad\quad$ 95 $\quad +$ 100 $\quad\quad\rule{2cm}{0.4pt}$ $\quad$ 460 $\div$ 5 $=$ 92

7.	
$\quad\quad$ 78 $\quad\quad$ 87 $\quad\quad$ 75 $\quad +$? $\quad\quad\rule{2cm}{0.4pt}$ $\quad$ 332 $\div$ 4 $=$ 83 **Bonus: ? = 92**	90-100 $\quad=\quad$ A 80-89 $\quad\quad=\quad$ B 74-79 $\quad\quad=\quad$ C 70-73 $\quad\quad=\quad$ D 69 and below is failing

ACTIVITY 3.3: The Two Book Bags Game

OBJECTIVE: Students will learn how to keep an organized and neat book bag.

MATERIALS: Two book bags:

Fill each one with some of the following items: Homework Folder, Text Books, Agenda, Paper, Pencil Case, Markers, Subject Worksheets, Pencils, Pens, and other various school supplies that would be in a student's book bag.

Make one book bag neat and organized with everything in its place.

Make the other book bag as messy as possible with loose papers, pencils on the bottom, markers in different places, etc.

Make sure both book bags have the same items in them.

PROCEDURES:

1. Tell students that they are going to play a game today. Begin by dividing the class into two teams by putting them on opposite sides of the room. Have them circle around a desk or table.

2. Tell students that you are going to give each team a book bag.

3. When you call out an item in the book bag (ones you put in there), have each team rush to find the item and bring it up to you. The first team to do so will receive a point for their team. Tell them not to dump out the bookbag.

4. Have two students on each team look in the book bag together for the item. When you call the next item, have each team switch students. (You can also have all the students look in the bookbag at once if you would like.)

5. Make sure you make it hard for the team with the messy book bag to find the items. The team with the neat book bag should get all or most of the points.

6. After calling out several items, the team with the messy book bag may catch on or wonder why the other team is finding the items so quickly. You may even hear them say it's not fair.

7. At this time, stop the game and have everyone return to their seats. Bring the two book bags to the front of the room. Show the students the difference between the two book bags by telling them that you made it easy for one team on purpose.

8. Ask students:
   - What made it easier for one team to find the items quickly?
   - How can keeping an organized book bag help you to do better in school?

SUMMARY: Remind students that it is important to keep all of their TOOLS organized so they will be able to find their homework and supplies easily.

ACTIVITY 3.4: Look at My Desk!

OBJECTIVE: Students will see how a clean and organized desk will help them find their Tools more quickly.

MATERIALS: Two students desks – one filled with school supplies and very messy and one empty desk with the school supplies on top of it.

Various school supply items for that grade level or classroom.

Reproducible – Look at My Desk! (one for each student)

PROCEDURES:

1. Show students the messy desk. Ask students what they see. Ask them how having a disorganized desk can affect their grades. They may not be able to find their assignments and therefore not get credit for them. If they don't get turned in, students may receive a zero for their grade on that assignment.

2. Put an empty desk in front of the room (on top of a table if you can so students can see what you are doing better).

3. Put all the school supplies needed for that class on top of the empty desk or nearby so you can easily get to them.

4. Have one student come up and put one of the items in the desk where it should be.

5. Continue by having another student come up and put an item in the desk until all the items are neatly organized in the desk.

6. Show students the messy desk again. Ask students which desk they would rather have at school. Tell students that it takes discipline to keep your desk organized. It means that when you have a piece of paper it needs to have a home. Tell students to think; does this paper go in a subject folder or the homework folder or can it be thrown away. It does not get shoved into the desk to find months later when it is too late to turn in for credit.

7. Distribute Reproducible – Look at My Desk! to all students.

8. As a class, name all the supplies needed for that class on the lines. Remember that each teacher may require different supplies so make sure to include only those items.

ACTIVITY 3.4: Look at My Desk!

CONTINUED...

9. Have students draw their organized desk with those items in it.

10. Tell students to keep this drawing in their homework folder to pull out a month later to see if it still looks organized. If their desk does not look organized, they have a picture of what it should look like that they can go by.

11. Depending on time, have students start organizing their desks according to their picture.

SUMMARY: Remind students that an organized desk is a habit that will help them to find their Tools better and not lose important assignments.

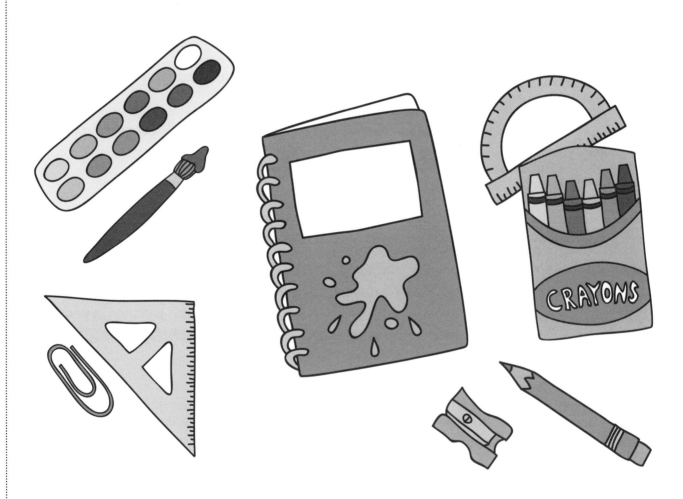

Look at My Desk!

Name: _____

DIRECTIONS: List all the TOOLS (school supplies) needed in your class below. Draw those items on top of the open desk below so it is organized. (This is how it would look inside the desk.)

1. _____
2. _____
3. _____
4. _____
5. _____

6. _____
7. _____
8. _____
9. _____
10. _____

11. _____
12. _____
13. _____
14. _____
15. _____

ACTIVITY 3.5: Who is Checking My Desk?

OBJECTIVE: To make sure students are keeping their SPACE and TOOLS at school neat and organized.

MATERIALS: Reproducible- Who is Checking My Desk cut apart
(This is a great addition to Extension Activity 3.4- Look at My Desk)

PROCEDURES:

1. Tell students that sometime during the week someone will be checking their desks to see if they are neat and organized. Say to students, "I wonder who will be checking your desk this week?"

2. Ask students how keeping a neat and organized desk will help you at school? Some answers are:
   - You will be able to find your books and folders
   - Assignments won't be lost
   - Papers will stay neat and not crumpled up

3. Let students know that if their desk is perfectly clean and organized, the desk fairy will leave them a treat. If their desk is messy, the desk monster may come to visit.

4. When the students are not in the classroom, check their desks and leave the appropriate "Note" and treat if applicable.

5. Once you have checked all the students' desks, talk about what you can do to keep your SPACE clean and neat and your TOOLS organized.

6. In future weeks you can say to the class, "I wonder who will be checking your desks this week?" The students will then know that they will be receiving one of the three notes.

7. Optional: Have a class ice-cream or popcorn party if the whole class earns a Desk Fairy.

SUMMARY: Let students know that it is important to keep your study SPACE neat and clean and their TOOLS organized at school and at home. That way they can find their materials and they don't have a messy desk distracting them.

Who is Checking My Desk?

Congratulations!
Your desk is neat and organized too.
So I'm leaving a little surprise for you!

The Desk Fairy

Congratulations!
Your desk is neat and organized too.
So I'm leaving a little surprise for you!

The Desk Fairy

Not too bad,
just a little cleaning and
you will be glad.

Not too bad,
Just a little cleaning and
you will be glad.

Uh Oh!
Please clean your desk
So I won't eat your mess!

The Desk Monster

Uh Oh!
Please clean your desk
So I won't eat your mess!

The Desk Monster

ACTIVITY 3.6: What's My Schedule?

OBJECTIVE: Students will practice making a homework schedule after school.

MATERIALS: Reproducible – What's My Schedule Scenarios (cut apart)

Reproducible – What's My Schedule Time Sheet (one for each group)

Reproducible – My Homework Schedule (one for each student, laminated if possible)

PROCEDURES:

1. Ask students the following questions:
   - How many of you play sports or have other after school commitments?
   - Have you ever not had enough time to do your homework at night because of your after school commitments?
   - How many of you have a set time or schedule to do your homework?
   - What do you do to fit everything in for the day?

2. Tell students that they are going to practice making an after school schedule.

3. Divide the class into six groups or the number of groups that work best for the class.

4. Distribute one "What's My Schedule" Scenario card and a "What's My Schedule" Time Sheet to each group.

5. Have each group read the scenario card and write a schedule on the time sheet that would work best for the student on the card. This will go from the time that student finishes school until bed time. You can remind the groups to include dinner, free time activities, and taking a bath or shower or you can let them try it first to see what schedule they come up with and then remind them of those later.

6. When they are finished, have each group read their scenario to the class and the schedule they came up with for the student. Ask the class if there is anything the group may have forgotten or if it sounds like a good schedule.

7. There is no set schedule for each scenario. Discuss the importance of getting the homework completed and how to use time wisely. It may be that the students on the cards have to start their homework right away without taking a break when they get home.

8. Distribute My Homework Schedule to each student.

CONTINUED...

9. Tell students that every day may be different due to their after school commitments, but it is important to have a set study time. Show students the two lines on the My Homework Schedule sheet. Have students think about their week and the time they will need to do their homework each day. On the first line have them write down the time they need to start their homework for that day. If they have enough time to finish their work then leave the second line blank. If they have an after school commitment and need to finish their homework later, write that time on the second line. This can be done at home.

10. For example, Anna on the scenario card may put 3:30 pm-5:00 pm on the first line and 8:30 pm-9:30 pm on the second line for Monday. Since she knows she has a busy schedule she gets to work right away. For Tuesday, she may put 4:00 pm-6:00 pm and then 7:30 pm-8:30 pm because she doesn't have any after school commitments. She can plan some free time activities or even work on homework that is due later on in the week.

11. If possible, laminate these for the students so they can change it from week to week if needed. Tell the students that they would need to get a wipe-off marker. If not, tell the students that they can use this one as a sample and make their own schedule on a piece of paper each week.

SUMMARY: Remind students that when they know the amount of time they need to do their homework, they will be more productive. It is easy to waste time without a schedule.

What's My Schedule Scenarios?

DIRECTIONS: Copy and cut-out the cards below (laminate for durability). Divide the class into small groups. Give each group a card and have them write out a schedule for that person using the What's My Schedule Time Sheet.

Johnny gets home from school at 3:30pm. He has soccer practice from 6:00pm to 7:30pm. Johnny also has some chores to do after school. He must walk the dog and do the dishes. He has a science test tomorrow, a math worksheet to complete, and a book report due in a week.

School gets out at 4:00pm. Katie is going to stay after school today for a help session in math. Her mom will pick her up at 5:00pm. Katie has a math and science test tomorrow and a reading log due. She needs to read 30 minutes every night and write a summary about what she read. Katie's five year old younger brother also looks forward to Katie playing with him after school.

Today is Monday. Anna gets home from school at 3:30pm. She has gymnastic practice from 5:30pm to 7:30pm. Her gym is about 15 minutes away. Anna has math homework due tomorrow, a science worksheet to finish, and a social studies test on Wednesday. She also needs to clean the kitchen before going to bed at 9:30pm.

School gets out at 3:00pm. Derek has band practice after school today. He gets home at 5:30pm. Derek has a science project due in one week that he hasn't started. He also has math homework that is due tomorrow and a social studies test in two days. Derek's friend wants him to ride bikes with him after school too.

Taylor has lacrosse practice after school from 3:00pm to 4:30pm. She has a science test tomorrow and a social studies worksheet due. She also has to read chapters 7 and 8 for her class book discussion tomorrow in language arts. Taylor is always in bed by 9:00pm.

Jacob is in high school and gets home at 3:00pm. He meets his little sister at the bus stop at 3:30pm. She is in 2nd grade. Jacob is responsible for watching his little sister until dad gets home at 6:00pm. He has a language arts assignment due tomorrow and a calculus test. Jacob loves language arts, but struggles with calculus. Jacob also has to cook dinner and help his sister with her homework.

What's My Schedule Time Sheet

Name: _____

3:00pm	_____	6:30pm	_____
3:30pm	_____	7:00pm	_____
4:00pm	_____	7:30pm	_____
4:30pm	_____	8:00pm	_____
5:00pm	_____	8:30pm	_____
5:30pm	_____	9:00pm	_____
6:00pm	_____	9:30pm	_____

What's My Schedule Time Sheet

Name: _____

3:00pm	_____	6:30pm	_____
3:30pm	_____	7:00pm	_____
4:00pm	_____	7:30pm	_____
4:30pm	_____	8:00pm	_____
5:00pm	_____	8:30pm	_____
5:30pm	_____	9:00pm	_____
6:00pm	_____	9:30pm	_____

Homework Schedule

Monday	Tuesday	Wednesday	Thursday	Friday
Time:	Time:	Time:	Time:	Time:
_____	_____	_____	_____	_____
_____	_____	_____	_____	_____

Homework Schedule

Monday	Tuesday	Wednesday	Thursday	Friday
Time:	Time:	Time:	Time:	Time:
_____	_____	_____	_____	_____
_____	_____	_____	_____	_____

ACTIVITY 3.7: Career Tools Game

OBJECTIVE: Students will identify the tools needed for various careers.

MATERIALS: Reproducible – Career Tools Game Cards (cut apart)
One piece of construction paper in four colors: Red, Blue, Orange, Green

PROCEDURES:

1. Preparation: Put each of the colored pieces of construction paper in the four corners of the room like it is laid out on the Career Tools Game Cards.

2. Tell students that they are going to play a game today about the Tools needed for various careers.

3. Have all the students stand up. Tell them that you are going to name a career and four tools that go with that profession. For each tool, point to the colored corner where that tool goes. For example, on the Doctor Card, tell students to go to the Red Corner for Stethoscope, the Blue Corner for Syringe, the Orange Corner for White Coat, and the Green Corner for Tongue Depressor.

4. Send two students outside the door so they cannot hear what career and tools are being said in the classroom.

5. While the two students are outside, read off a career and tools on the card by pointing to each colored corner for that tool. Have students decide which colored corner they would like to go to for the game (all students should be in one of the four corners). Tell students that they want to pick a corner (Tool) that they think the two students outside won't name.

6. Bring the two students back in the room. Ask each one to name a tool for the career on the card. (For example, on the doctor card, ask what are the tools of a doctor. If they say "white coat" everyone in the orange corner will sit down.)

7. Discuss that career. Have students name some more tools that go with that career. Ask students why those tools are important for that career.

8. Play another round with the remaining students as indicated above. See how many students are left. Once again, discuss the career on the card.

9. After the second round, have everyone play again by sending two more students out of the room and naming a career and its tools. Continue play for another round with the remaining students and then start over again with all the students.

SUMMARY: Tell students that every profession needs certain tools to be successful.

Career Tools

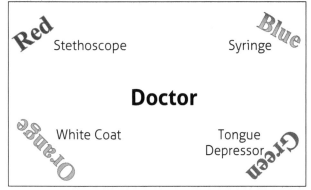

Red — Stethoscope
Blue — Syringe

Doctor

Orange — White Coat
Green — Tongue Depressor

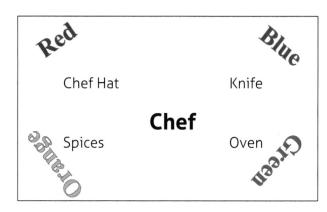

Red — Chef Hat
Blue — Knife

Chef

Orange — Spices
Green — Oven

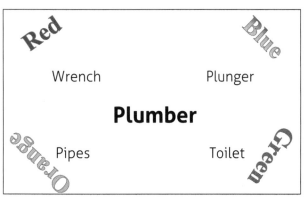

Red — Wrench
Blue — Plunger

Plumber

Orange — Pipes
Green — Toilet

Red — Scissors
Blue — Thread

Tailor

Orange — Sewing Machine
Green — Fabric

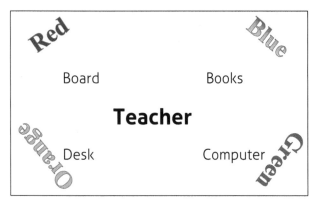

Red — Board
Blue — Books

Teacher

Orange — Desk
Green — Computer

Red — Lawnmower
Blue — Rake

Yard Person

Orange — Trimmers
Green — Hose

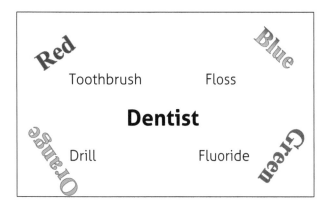

Red — Toothbrush
Blue — Floss

Dentist

Orange — Drill
Green — Fluoride

Red — Scanner
Blue — Money

Cashier

Orange — Cash Register
Green — Uniform

Career Tools

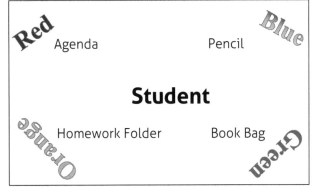

Red Agenda Pencil **Blue**

Student

Orange Homework Folder Book Bag **Green**

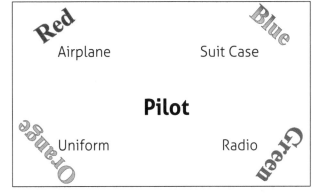

Red Airplane Suit Case **Blue**

Pilot

Orange Uniform Radio **Green**

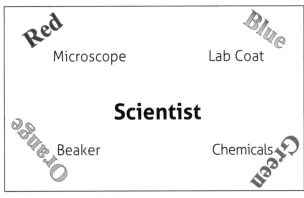

Red Microscope Lab Coat **Blue**

Scientist

Orange Beaker Chemicals **Green**

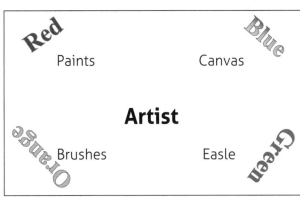

Red Paints Canvas **Blue**

Artist

Orange Brushes Easle **Green**

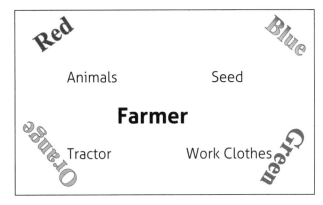

Red Animals Seed **Blue**

Farmer

Orange Tractor Work Clothes **Green**

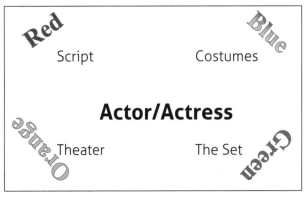

Red Script Costumes **Blue**

Actor/Actress

Orange Theater The Set **Green**

Red Marked Car Handcuffs **Blue**

Police Officer

Orange Gun Badge **Green**

Red Stick Mouth Guard **Blue**

Lacrosse Player

Orange Uniform Ball **Green**

ACTIVITY 3.8: Tools Survey

OBJECTIVE: Students will identify their organizational strengths and weaknesses.

MATERIALS: Reproducible- Tools Survey (one for each student)

PROCEDURES:

1. Distribute Reproducible – Tools Survey to each student.

2. Have each student take the survey according to the directions.

3. When they have finished, have them add up the numbers to get a total score. Have students look at the key based on the number they added up.

4. Read and discuss each survey statement. Ask students why each of these is important to being a successful student.

5. Have students circle the two statements that they scored the highest on in the survey. Ask students what they do to keep that score high.

6. Have students cross out the two statements that they scored the lowest on in the survey. Ask all students for each statement what they could do to improve in that area.

7. Have students write down one suggestion, for each low scored statement, for how to improve in that area.

SUMMARY: Remind students that they are learning habits that will help them to do better in school. Staying organized and using the necessary tools appropriately will help students feel better prepared in school.

Tools Survey

DIRECTIONS: Complete the survey by circling the appropriate number that is indicated. Add up your points to see how you scored at the bottom.

		Always	Often	Sometimes	Rarely	Never
1.	I am organized.	5	4	3	2	1
2.	I use my agenda to write down assignments.	5	4	3	2	1
3.	I put my completed assignments in my homework folder so they are ready to turn in.	5	4	3	2	1
4.	My desk is organized.	5	4	3	2	1
5.	I use my Toolbox at home so I do not have to get up to find something.	5	4	3	2	1
6.	My book bag is organized and clean.	5	4	3	2	1
7.	I use a homework schedule so I know how much time I have to complete my homework after school.	5	4	3	2	1
8.	I bring the necessary books and materials home with me.	5	4	3	2	1
9.	I have all the necessary tools I need at school.	5	4	3	2	1
10.	I put papers away in their designated folders.	5	4	3	2	1
Total:						

46+   Excellent! You really use your time wisely.

40-45   Good job! You use your time pretty well.

34-39   Okay! You need some help in a few areas.

25-33   Looks like there are several areas that need improvement.

10-29   Let's talk!

My Score is: _____

1. Circle the two areas above where you scored the highest. Great job!

2. X-Out the two areas that need the most improvement.

3. What can you do to make improvements on the ones you crossed out? _____

_____

ACTIVITY 3.9: Name That Tool Crossword

OBJECTIVE: Students will name the tools of a student by using the given clues.

MATERIALS: Reproducible – Name that Tool Crossword

PROCEDURES:

1. Distribute Reproducible – Name that Tool Crossword to each student.

2. Have students work independently on the puzzle for five minutes.

3. After five minutes, tell the students that they can work with another student on the puzzle if they would like.

4. When the students have finished, go over each statement by asking what answer they put down in the puzzle.

SUMMARY: Remind students about the importance of keeping their tools organized at school and at home.

Created on TheTeachersCorner.net
Crossword Maker

Name That Tool Crossword

Name: _____

DIRECTIONS: Complete the crossword below.

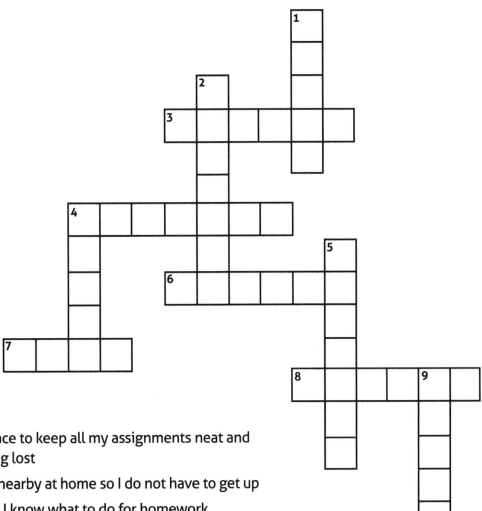

Across
3. This is a place to keep all my assignments neat and from getting lost

4. I keep this nearby at home so I do not have to get up

6. This is how I know what to do for homework

7. A place to put my tools in at school

8. This is made of wood and lead

Down
1. I do my assignments on this

2. This is used to bring all my tools to and from school

4. The supplies a student needs to be successful

5. I use these to make my assignments more colorful

9. I use these cards to make flashcards to help me study

*Created on TheTeachersCorner.net
Crossword Maker*

Name That Tool Crossword

Name: _____

DIRECTIONS: Complete the crossword below.

```
                              ¹p
                               a
                        ²b     p
                     ³f  o  l  d  e  r
                        o        r
                        k
              ⁴t  o  o  l  b  o  x
               o           a        ⁵m
               o        ⁶a  g  e  n  d  a
               l                    r
              ⁷d  e  s  k           k
                                 ⁸p  e  n  c  ⁹i  l
                                  r           n
                                  s           d
                                              e
                                              x
```

Across

3. This is a place to keep all my assignments neat and from getting lost

4. I keep this nearby at home so I do not have to get up

6. This is how I know what to do for homework

7. A place to put my tools in at school

8. This is made of wood and lead

Down

1. I do my assignments on this

2. This is used to bring all my tools to and from school

4. The supplies a student needs to be successful

5. I use these to make my assignments more colorful

9. I use these cards to make flashcards to help me study

Created on TheTeachersCorner.net
Crossword Maker

{Session Four}

Ending

Goal Setting and Prioritizing

Overview: Every goal must have a beginning before it can reach the ending. Even Stephen Covey talked about having the end in mind with what you want to be and do. For students, it is important to learn how to set both academic and personal long and short-term goals. And it is also important to learn how to break a long-term goal down into shorter goals. When students learn how to create SMART goals and achieve them, they will then feel successful and truly own their learning.

ENDING Contents:

ENDING Parent Letter (Included on CD)

Core Lesson 4 • E- ENDING

Activity 4.1 • Beginning to Ending

Activity 4.2 • Breaking Down the Goal

Activity 4.3 • Now and Later

Activity 4.4 • Long and Short

Activity 4.5 • The Future is Mine!

Activity 4.6 • Goal Collage

Activity 4.7 • My SMART Goals

Activity 4.8 • Number Fun

Activity 4.9 • Hoola-Hoop Bustle

Activity 4.10 • Nothing is Impossible

CORE LESSON 4: "E" – Ending

OBJECTIVE: Students will learn the importance of setting goals.

MATERIALS: Beach Ball

PROCEDURES:

1. Draw the steps on the board like picture A below. Put the letter "S" and the word SPACE on the first step like in picture B. Review by asking students what they remember about the letter "S" for SPACE. (It is to keep their study SPACE at home free from distractions). Put the letter "T" and the word TOOLS on the second step. Ask students what they remember about the letter "T" for TOOLS. (A Toolbox is needed at home so they do not have to get up. And the two most important tools of a student are their agenda and homework folder).

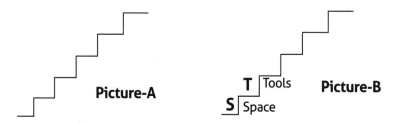

2. Introduce the letter "E" by writing the letter "E" on the next step and the word ENDING by it like picture C below. Tell students that to get to where they would like to go; they need to start at the beginning before they can get to the ending. Just like a set of stairs, they need to start at the first step before they can get to the top. Tell students that ENDING is like a goal.

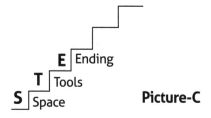

3. Ask students what is a goal. Discuss answers. It is something that you are trying to achieve. Tell students that goals can be personal, academic, and career-oriented. For example, a personal goal is to eat more fruits and vegetables. An academic goal is improve your math grade. And a career-oriented goal may be to become a lawyer. They can also be long-term or short-term.

CORE LESSON 4: "E" – Ending

CONTINUED...

4. Ask students to give you examples of short-term goals and then long-term goals. Some ideas are:
   - Make the school swim team this year: Short-term
   - Graduate from high school: Long-term
   - Learn to play chess: Short-term
   - Travel to Europe: Long or Short-term
   - Improve my social studies grade: Short-term
   - Become a computer technician: Long-term
   - Learn my multiplication facts: Short-term

5. Put the word SMART lengthwise on the board. Tell students that goals should be SMART goals.

   S –Specific: Ask students why goals should be Specific. It tells us what we want to accomplish.

   M – Measureable: Ask students why goals should be Measureable. It is so we will know that our goal was accomplished; we reached our goal.

   A – Achievable: Ask students why goals should be Achievable. It is how the goal will be accomplished. It is the plan.

   R – Realistic: Ask students why goals should be Realistic. Is this goal really attainable? For instance, it is not a realistic goal to become an Olympic gymnast at the age of 40.

   T – Timely: Ask students why goals should be Timely. They need to have an ending or due date.

6. Activity:
   - Have students stand up by their desk.
     - Tell them that we are going to make a SMART goal by trying to keep the beach ball in the air for 20 hits without it dropping.
     - Ask students if this goal is Specific. Yes, we know what we want to accomplish.
     - Ask students if this goal is Measureable. Yes, if we reach 20 we have accomplished our goal.
     - Ask students if the goal is Achievable. Yes, it is. Ask them if they have a plan for keeping it in the air. Students may say not to hit it so hard that another person cannot get it. Discuss any other ideas.
     - Ask students if the goal is Realistic. Yes, it is possible to keep the ball in the air 20 times.
     - Ask students if the goal is Timely. Yes, it should only take a couple minutes to accomplish this goal.
   - Throw the ball in the air and start counting for every person who hits the ball.
   - Discuss the results.

SUMMARY: Ask students what they learned about setting goals today.

ACTIVITY 4.1: Beginning to Ending

- **OBJECTIVE:** Students will learn the process of accomplishing a goal.

MATERIALS: Reproducible 4.2 – Beginning to Ending (Cut out and sorted by topic. It is best to copy them on cardstock and laminate them for durability)

Dry erase board or SMART Board

PROCEDURES:

1. Tell students that every day they start and finish tasks without even knowing it. Ask students if they thought about getting dressed this morning. Most will answer no. They just got up and got dressed. Tell students that they didn't think about putting their shirt on, then their pants, and then their socks, etc., they just did it, but there were steps involved for getting ready.

2. Tell students that some activities or goals do not take any thought and they can just do them, but some tasks need to be planned out from beginning to ending.

3. Draw steps on the board like the picture below. Put one set of topic cards mixed up on the board (they can either be taped or clipped up there or you can put a magnet on the back of each card). Tell students that their goal is to get to the last step or the end.

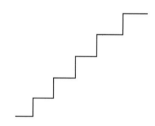

4. Have one student come up and pick what he/she thinks would be the first step for that topic. Have the student put it on the first STEP on the board.

5. Continue by having the other students come up to the board and put the next step in the sequence for that topic on the STEPS.

6. Some of the topics have a definite sequence, like doing the laundry. But for some of the other topics one step can interchange with another step in the sequence. For example, eating healthy for trying out for basketball can be any place in the sequence or you may want to practice your 6-10 multiplication facts before the 1-5 facts. Discuss with the students that when you make a plan, allow for some flexibility. Also, when they have a book report they may choose to draw the illustrations before the writing the rough copy or vice versa. However, tell the students that they cannot write the book report before reading the book.

7. Continue with the other topic sets the same way for the time allowed.

SUMMARY: Remind students that some goals take more thought to go from beginning to ending.

Doing the Laundry

Get dirty clothes from your hamper.	Sort your clothes by color.
Decide on which color to wash first in the washing machine.	Load the washing machine.
Put the soap in the washing machine.	Turn the washing machine on to start.
Put the washed clothes in the dryer.	Fold and put away the clean clothes.

[Making a Peanut Butter and Jelly Sandwich]

Get two pieces of bread.	Get out the peanut butter and jelly.
Spread the peanut butter on one piece of bread.	Spread the jelly on the other piece of bread.
Put the two pieces of bread together.	Enjoy your peanut butter and jelly sandwich.

[Doing the Dishes]

Bring the dishes from the kitchen table to the counter.	Scrape leftover food into the trash can.

Beginning to Ending

Load the dishes into the dishwasher.	Put soap into the dispenser.
Turn the dishwasher on.	Unload the dishwasher into the cupboards.

[Try Out for the Basketball Team]

Decide that you would like to play basketball.	Practice every day after school until try outs.
Eat healthy.	Sign up for basketball try outs.

Beginning to Ending

Try out for the basketball team.

Congratulations! You made the basketball team!

[Learn Your Multiplication Facts]

Get a set of flashcards.

Quiz yourself with the 1-5 multiplication fact cards.

Make one pile of 1-5 cards that you know and another pile of ones you do not know.

Continue with the 1-5 multiplication fact cards until you know all of them.

Quiz yourself with the 6-10 multiplication fact cards.

Make one pile of 6-10 cards that you know and another pile of ones you do not know.

Continue with the 6-10 multiplication fact cards until you know all of them.

Quiz yourself with all of the multiplication fact cards.

Review your multiplication fact cards every week to make sure you know them.

Yea! You learned your multiplication facts.

[Doing Your Homework]

Have a snack when you get home.

Take books and agenda out of book bag.

Get your Toolbox out.

Clean your study SPACE so it is free from distractions.

Look in your agenda to see what assignments are due.

Do your hardest subject first.

Put your hardest subject in your Homework Folder.

Do your easiest subject.

Put your easiest assignment in your Homework Folder.

Pack up your book bag.

Put your book bag by the door for the morning.

Go and have fun!

ACTIVITY 4.2: Breaking Down the Goal!

OBJECTIVE: Students will learn to break down the steps of a goal.

MATERIALS: Reproducible – What a Fun Day Book Report (one for each student)

Reproducible – Breaking Down the Goal Worksheet (one for a group of 4-5 students)

Reproducible – Breaking Down the Goal Calendar (one for a group of 4-5 students)

PROCEDURES:

1. Ask students: Have you ever done a book report? Could you read the book and write the report in one day?

2. Tell students that a book report takes time to complete because there are a lot of steps to do.

3. Tell students that we are going to practice breaking down a book report so they can see all the steps involved. This will also help them in the future.

4. Divide students into groups of 4-5 students. Distribute Reproducibles: What a Fun Day! Book Report, Breaking Down the Goal Worksheet, and Breaking Down the Goal Calendar.

5. Tell students that their teacher assigned them a book report and it is due March 31st (write that on the board). The details for the book report are on the sheet titled, "What a Fun Day!" Have students read the details for the book report and then have the group make a list of what needs to be completed on the Breaking Down the Goal Worksheet. Remind students not to forget steps such as finding a book, reading the book, writing a rough draft, etc. The rubric is also helpful for making sure all the details are covered because that is how students are graded.

6. Once the groups have completed the Breaking Down the Goal Worksheet, have them share by discussing each step. Have them add additional steps on their paper if another group mentioned a step they would like to add.

   Possible STEPS:
   • Find a book at the library
   • Read chapters 1-3 (Note: reading the book can be broken down even further)
   • Read chapters 4-6
   • Read chapters 7-10
   • Read chapters 11-14
   • Write an outline
   • Write the five paragraph essay rough draft
   • Type the final copy
   • Glue the final copy on the left side of the poster board and write the title above it.
   • Draw the illustrations in the middle of the poster board

ACTIVITY 4.2: Breaking Down the Goal!

CONTINUED...

- Complete the right side of the poster board by writing the title, author's name, and your name in marker.
- Write the rough draft of your thoughts about the book.
- Type the final copy of your thoughts about the book.
- Glue the final copy of your thoughts about the book on the right side of the poster below your name.
- Turn your book report in to the teacher by March 31st.

Note: All 15 steps do not need to be filled in on the worksheet. It only gives students a picture of how a goal could be broken down.

7. Discuss with the students that this is just a list of possible STEPS. Each one mentioned above may be broken down even further. For instance, students may say that they are going to read chapters 1-3 in one day or they may break it down and read two on one day and the last one on another.

8. Tell students they are now going to put the STEPS on the calendar. Tell them that today is March 1st. Have students write the due date on the calendar. Ask students how many days do they have to complete their book report. (Note: This can also be done as an entire class.)

9. Have the groups fill in the calendar with the steps from their Breaking Down the Goal Worksheet. Have students think about how long certain tasks will take and allow for that time.

10. Have each group come to the front of the room and share how they broke down their goal from beginning to ending.

SUMMARY: Remind students that the next time they are assigned a book report to think of all the steps involved and plan them out on a calendar.

What a Fun Day! Book Report

What if you could spend the day with a character in the book you read? What would you do for the day? For this book report, you will create a tri-fold poster describing your day with one of the characters in your book.

MATERIALS:

Poster board cut in a 12x24 size
Markers, crayons, paper, glue sticks

DIRECTIONS:

1. Find a book that is appropriate for your reading level.

2. Cut your poster board so that it is 12x24 inches.

3. Fold your poster board so that it is in thirds.

4. On the left side of your poster, glue a one page typed paper of at least five paragraphs describing the adventure you had with your character. Be sure to include details on where you went and what you did. Write with a marker a title for your essay on the poster board above the essay.

5. In the middle of the poster, draw an illustration of you and your character in a scene from your day together. Do not use computer images. All drawings must be completed by hand.

6. On the right side of your poster, write the name of the book, the author's name, your name, and type a brief description of why you liked or did not like your book. Glue your description below your name.

SCORING RUBRIC:

	Possible Points Earned
1. Did you turn your book report poster in on time?	5
2. Did you include a five paragraph essay on the left side of the poster?	10
3. Was there detailed information in your essay describing your day with the character?	30
4. Did you include an illustration in the center part of the poster?	25
5. On the right side of your poster, did you include the required information?	10
6. Is the grammar, spelling, and punctuation correct?	10
7. Was your poster neat and organized correctly?	10

Breaking Down the Goal Worksheet

DIRECTIONS:

After reading the "What a Fun Day Book Report" requirements, break down the parts to be completed on the STEPS below. Note: You do not need to fill in all 15 steps.

1. STEP One: _____

2. STEP Two: _____

3. STEP Three: _____

4. STEP Four: _____

5. STEP Five: _____

6. STEP Six: _____

7. STEP Seven: _____

8. STEP Eight: _____

9. STEP Nine: _____

10. STEP Ten: _____

11. STEP Eleven: _____

12. STEP Twelve: _____

13. STEP Thirteen: _____

14. STEP Fourteen: _____

15. STEP Fifteen: _____

March Calendar

MARCH

Sunday	Monday	Tuesday	Wednesday	Thursday	Friday	Saturday

ACTIVITY 4.3: Now and Later

OBJECTIVE: Students will learn to prioritize homework assignments and activities after school.

MATERIALS: Reproducible 4.3 – Now and Later (one for each student)
Now and Later Candy (optional)

PROCEDURES:

1. Review with students that when they set a goal, there are often several steps involved to achieving that goal.

2. Ask students if they have ever seen their parent make a "To Do" list at home. For example, your parent/guardian may make a list of what he/she is going to do this weekend. He/she may need to mow the lawn, fix the fence, go to the grocery store, pay the bills, go to your game, cook dinner, etc.

3. Tell students that sometimes we may need to prioritize our list. Ask students what the word prioritize means. It means to arrange the items in order of importance. Their parent/guardian will prioritize what needs to be done first, then second, and so forth until he/she has completed the "To Do" list.

4. Discuss with students that it often helps to complete the harder task or assignment first while leaving the easiest task for later. Ask students why they might think this is a good idea. Harder subjects may take longer to complete so it is best to start with those assignments knowing the easiest ones will not take as long.

5. Discuss with students that it is also important to complete tasks that are due sooner than later. Ask students if it is Monday and they have a test on Friday, but they also have a math worksheet due on Tuesday, which one should they work on first? They should pick the math worksheet because it is due tomorrow.

6. Distribute Reproducible 4.3- Now and Later to all students. Tell students that these are assignments in their agendas for homework.

7. Have students rank order the subjects by using #1 as the first subject to complete, #2 as the second subject to complete, and so on. For example, in number 1 social studies is the hardest subject so it should have the # 1 next to it to do that subject first.

8. Let students know that there may be some choice with the rankings. Tell students that they may have the subject ranked differently than another student in their class and that is fine.

9. Tell students that all subjects are due the next day unless it is noted.

10. Discuss the rankings for each one.

ACTIVITY 4.3: Now and Later

CONTINUED...

- For the first one, social studies would be ranked #1, math and reading log could be ranked #2 or #3 depending on what they would like to do next, but they should study for the spelling test last because it isn't until Thursday.

- For the second one, they have until the tennis match to complete all their homework for the weekend. Unfinished homework should be #1, the science worksheet should be #2, and they should work on their book report until they leave for the tennis match at 2:00pm.

- Continue discussing the rest of the rankings.

SUMMARY: Remind students that it is important to prioritize their assignments and activities. (Optional) As a treat, you can give them a "Now and Later" candy at the end of the lesson to remind them to do some assignments now and others later.

Now and Later

DIRECTIONS:

Rank each of the following lists below by using #1 as the first task to complete, #2 being the second task to complete, and so on. All subjects are in your agenda and due the next day unless noted.

1. It is Tuesday night and social studies is your hardest subject.

    _____ Social studies worksheet

    _____ Math homework p.38

    _____ Reading log

    _____ Spelling test on Thursday

2. It is Saturday. You only have until your tennis match to do all your homework.

    _____ Tennis match at 2:00pm

    _____ Book report due next Friday

    _____ Unfinished homework due Monday

    _____ Science worksheet

3. It is Monday night and math is your favorite subject.

    _____ Science test on Thursday

    _____ Reading worksheet p. 49

    _____ Math pp. 36-39

    _____ Book report due Friday

4. It's Wednesday night.

    _____ Soccer practice at 6pm

    _____ Art project due Friday

    _____ Reading worksheet

    _____ Spelling test

5. It is Tuesday night. Science is your favorite subject.

    _____ Science worksheet

    _____ Book report rough draft due Thursday

    _____ Language arts worksheet

    _____ Piano practice at 4:30pm

6. It is Thursday night and math is your hardest subject.

    _____ Gymnastics from 6-8pm

    _____ Read chapters 1-3 for reading

    _____ Decide on historical figure for book report

    _____ Math homework p. 78

7. It is Monday night and reading is your hardest subject.

    _____ Read chapter 3 in social studies book

    _____ Math homework p. 67

    _____ Illustrations for book report

    _____ Science worksheet due Wednesday

8. It is Tuesday night.

    _____ Book report is due Friday

    _____ Science homework p. 45

    _____ Reading log

    _____ Lacrosse practice from 5-7pm

ACTIVITY 4.4: Long Term and Short Term Goals

OBJECTIVE: Students will learn to identify long and short-term goals.

MATERIALS: Reproducible – Long and Short

PROCEDURES:

1. Tell students that goals can be long or short. It may take a day or a month or longer to achieve a goal depending on what it is.

2. Have students give you an example of a long-term goal. Have them give you an example of a short-term goal. (Long-term goal: Improve my math grade; Short-term goal: Practice my math facts every night for 20 minutes)

3. Distribute Reproducible – Long and Short to every student.

4. Have students put the letter "L" on the line if it is a long-term goal and the letter "S" if it is a short-term goal.

5. Discuss each one after the students have finished.

SUMMARY: Have students share a long and short-term goal they would like to work on for this month.

Long and Short

DIRECTIONS:

Mark the letter "L" on the line for long-term goal and the letter "S" for short-term goal. (Note: Each one could be the letter "S" or "L" depending on the time frame.)

1. _____ Improve my math grade.

2. _____ Study for my social studies test tonight.

3. _____ Practice my math facts for 30 minutes every night for a week.

4. _____ Turn in all my homework for this quarter.

5. _____ Compliment a friend today.

6. _____ Read four books this quarter.

7. _____ Improve my science grade.

8. _____ Practice playing tennis three times a week.

9. _____ Get a good conduct grade this quarter.

10. _____ Make more friends.

11. _____ Make the A/B Honor Roll for this quarter.

12. _____ Draw the illustrations for my book report this week.

13. _____ Raise my hand in class today.

14. _____ Read 30 minutes every night.

15. _____ Sell 100 Girl Scout Cookies.

16. _____ Turn my science project in on time.

17. _____ Make flashcards for my social studies test.

18. _____ Learn to play the piano.

ACTIVITY 4.5: The Future is Mine!

OBJECTIVE: Students will recognize the importance of setting goals.

MATERIALS: Reproducible – The Future is Mine! (one for each student)

PROCEDURES:

1. Ask students if they know more now than when they started school in kindergarten. Have students share some things they have accomplished up until now. Some answers are: learned to ride a bike, learned to play a sport, made the A-B honor roll, learned to read, etc.

2. Distribute reproducible – The Future is Mine to all students.

3. Tell students that today they are graduating from high school. They are about to walk up on stage to receive their diploma. While they are walking up to get their diploma, they start thinking about everything they have accomplished in life up until now.

4. Have students write or draw all the accomplishments they achieved. To help the students brainstorm have them think about personal and academic goals they would like to achieve. Some examples are: making the varsity soccer team, graduating with all A's and B's, was the lead in a play, was the captain of the debate team, learned to drive a car, volunteered at the local animal shelter once a month, tutored some elementary school children, went to the homecoming dance, joined the Key Club, worked at the grocery store, etc.

5. Have students share their accomplishments.

6. Tell students that goals start as dreams. And if these dreams are important, they need to make them happen.

7. Ask students if their goal was to be captain of the debate team, how can they accomplish that goal. Discuss answers. Ask students if they could start high school by being the captain. No, they would need to join a team first and then in a couple years be the captain.

SUMMARY: Remind students that the future is theirs if they only dream it.

The Future is Mine!

DIRECTIONS:

Pretend you are graduating from high school. You are about to walk up on stage to receive your diploma. You are thinking about all that you have accomplished in your life up until now. Write or draw these accomplishments in the thought bubbles.

ACTIVITY 4.6: Goal Collage

OBJECTIVE: Students will make a collage of their goals that they can hang up at home.

MATERIALS:

Construction paper (one for each student)

Magazines

Scissors

Glue

Markers

Art supplies

PROCEDURES:

1. Have students think about what they would like to accomplish in school and in life. Discuss answers. They can be academic goals, personal goals, or career goals.

2. Tell students that sometimes when they have a picture of their goals to look at; it will remind them of what they want to accomplish and what is important to them.

3. Distribute construction paper, magazines, and art supplies to the students.

4. Have them cut out inspirational words, pictures, etc. that would represent their goals. Option: If students are having a hard time finding specific pictures, tell them that they can print some out from the computer.

5. Have them glue their pictures and words onto their piece of construction paper. Students can decorate their collages with stickers, draw specific pictures, and even write their goals on the piece of construction paper.

6. Have students share their Goal Collages with the class.

SUMMARY: Remind students to put their collages up for them to see daily. This will remind them of their goals.

ACTIVITY 4.7: My SMART Goals

OBJECTIVE: Students will learn how to set short-term and long-term goals.

MATERIALS:

Reproducible – My SMART Goals, Reproducible- My SMART Goals Examples, Optional: File Folders

PROCEDURES:

1. Review SMART Goals with students. Ask students if they remember what each letter stands for in the word.

   S- Specific: What do we want to accomplish?
   M- Measureable: To know we reached our goal.
   A- Achievable: This is the plan.
   R- Realistic: Can you attain this goal?
   T- Timely: It has a due date.

2. Ask students why we have goals. Discuss answers.

3. Ask students to name some long-term goals. Tell students that to reach those long-term goals they need to be broken down into smaller goals which are short-term goals.

4. Distribute Reproducibles- My SMART Goals and My SMART Goals Examples to students.

5. Have students look at My SMART Goals Example sheet. Discuss examples of long and short-term goals. Have students see if they can match which short-term goal goes with the long-term goal.

6. Tell students to look at their My SMART Goals sheet. Have them write down a long-term academic and personal goal they would like to work on for this next month. Then have them break that goal down for the first week only. For example, the long-term goal may be to improve their reading grade. The first week's short-term goal may be to read for 30 minutes every night.

7. Tell the students at the beginning of the second week to have them evaluate their short-term goal to see if they reached it. They should then write their second week's goal. From the example above they may continue to read for 30 minutes or increase the time. They may also add to practice reading comprehension quizzes on the computer for their short-term goal.

8. Tell students to continue the same way for weeks three and four.

9. Optional: You can have them decorate a file folder to keep their goal sheet in for the month. After the month is up they can either staple another goal sheet on top of the first one or replace it.

SUMMARY: Ask students to share their long and short-term goals and what they think their next step should be in making sure they reach them.

My SMART Goals Examples

LONG-TERM ACADEMIC GOALS

- Improve my reading grade
- Improve my math grade
- Learn my multiplication facts
- Turn in all my homework for this quarter
- Turn in 90% of my homework this quarter
- Improve my science grade
- Improve my social studies grade
- Read x-amount of books this quarter
- Complete my book report or project on time
- Improve my language arts grade
- Improve my spelling grade
- Others:

LONG-TERM PERSONAL GOALS

- Improve my conduct grade for this quarter
- Make more friends
- Learn to play a sport
- Learn to play an instrument
- Have zero discipline referrals this quarter
- Have only one discipline referral this quarter or year
- Sing a solo in chorus
- Be a peer leader
- Raise money for a local animal shelter
- Try-out for the lacrosse team
- Achieve x-amount of Girl Scout/ Boy Scout badges
- Others:

SHORT-TERM ACADEMIC GOALS

- Break down my book report into steps
- Practice my math facts for 20 minutes every night
- Read for 30 minutes every night
- Turn in my homework every day for one week
- Write my spelling words 10 times every night until the test
- Read one book every two weeks
- Take one practice multiplication test a night
- Read my science study guide every night four days before the test
- Write neatly on my assignments
- Others:

SHORT-TERM PERSON GOALS

- Practice lacrosse every night until try-outs
- Do a random act of kindness every day
- Work on Girl Scout / Boy Scout badge part 1 this week
- Have a car wash this week to raise money for the animal shelter
- Give peer leader referrals out to teachers this week
- Practice playing soccer four times a week
- Raise my hand during class
- Compliment a friend every day
- Follow the teacher's directions the first time given
- Others:

My SMART Goals

MY ACADEMIC GOAL IS:

MY PERSONAL GOAL IS:

MY SHORT-TERM GOALS

WEEK 1:

I met my goal: YES / NO   If yes, YEA!

If no, what can I do differently for next week?

_____

I met my goal: YES / NO   If yes, YEA!

If no, what can I do differently for next week?

_____

WEEK 2:

I met my goal: YES / NO   If yes, YEA!

If no, what can I do differently for next week?

_____

I met my goal: YES / NO   If yes, YEA!

If no, what can I do differently for next week?

_____

WEEK 3:

I met my goal: YES / NO   If yes, YEA!

If no, what can I do differently for next week?

_____

I met my goal: YES / NO   If yes, YEA!

If no, what can I do differently for next week?

_____

WEEK 4:

I met my goal: YES / NO   If yes, YEA!

If no, what can I do differently for next week?

_____

I met my goal: YES / NO   If yes, YEA!

If no, what can I do differently for next week?

_____

ACTIVITY 4.8: Number Fun!

OBJECTIVE: Students will work together to accomplish a goal. Students will also learn the importance of being organized.

MATERIALS:

Reproducible – Number Fun! (Preparation: Copied and cut apart. It is best to laminate them for durability)

Stop Watch or Timer

Dry-erase Board or SMART Board

PROCEDURES:

1. Tape the numbers from Reproducible – Number Fun! up on the board all mixed up. Only put up enough numbers for the number of students in the room. You can also put magnets on the back of the numbers. (You can also write the numbers on the board in an unorganized way instead of using the Reproducible – Number Fun!)

2. Have the students stand up by their desks. Tell the students that you are going to time them to see how fast they can circle all the numbers in consecutive order on the board. Only one person can circle a number at a time.

3. Tell the students that you will hand the dry-erase marker to one student. Once that student circles #1, he/she will hand the marker to someone else in the room that will then circle #2, and so on until all the students have been to the board. Students who have circled a number will then sit down.

4. Ask the students before you begin if they would like to talk about the task as a class before you start.

5. When they are ready, hand the marker to a student and start the stop watch or timer.

6. Once everyone has circled a number, stop the timer and tell the students their time. Discuss how they did and if there is a more organized way to accomplish the task. Erase the circles from around the numbers and have the students try again by setting a lower time than what they made.

7. Continue a few more times. Each time have the students make a goal that is lower than the previous time. After each time discuss how they did and by asking if there is a more organized way to accomplish the task. (Optional: Mix up the numbers each time.)

8. Hint: If the students do not think of this idea you can prompt them by asking them if they could hand the marker to the same student each time so everyone has designated a number.

9. Tell the students that at the beginning there seemed to be a lot of chaos, but once they became more organized they were more efficient about achieving their goal, thus improving their time. Discuss how that relates to their school work.

SUMMARY: Remind students that they have to be organized to achieve their goals.

1	2	3
4	5	6
7	8	9
10	11	12

13	14	15
16	17	18
19	20	21
22	23	24

25	26	27
28	29	30
31	32	33
34	35	36

ACTIVITY 4.9: Hoola-Hoop Bustle

OBJECTIVE: Students will experience setting a goal with the Hoola-Hoops and working together to achieve it.

MATERIALS:

Two Hoola-Hoops
A Clock or watch with a second hand or a stopwatch

PROCEDURES:

1. Have students form a circle in the classroom. It is best if you have an open space that will allow for movement.

2. Tell students that the object of this game is to set a goal for how long it will take them to get the hoola-hoop around the circle and back to the starting position while holding hands.

3. Ask students how fast they think they can get the hoola-hoop around the circle. Discuss times and agree on one as a class. (ex. 2 minutes, 5 minutes, 30 seconds, etc.)

4. Tell students to hold hands in a circle. Have two students hold hands through the hoola-hoop. When you say go, start the stopwatch. If students let go of their hands, start the game over again. (Tell students that sometimes goals are hard and they may need to start over with them or re-evaluate their goal).

5. Once the hoola-hoop has made it around the circle ask students the following:
   - Did you make your goal?
   - If you made your goal, how did it feel?
   - If you did not make your goal, what could you do differently next time?
   - Do you need to change the agreed upon time, or set a new goal?

6. Have students try again with the same goal or a new goal. Ask students the same questions as above in number 5. Continue a couple more times until they reach their goal.

7. Now tell the students that you are going to put two hoola-hoops in the circle. Have the class set a goal for the amount of time it will take them to get two hoola-hoops around the circle going in opposite directions.

8. Once the hoola-hoops have made it around the circle ask students the following:
   - How were the two goals different?
   - What made this activity harder than the one with only one hoola-hoop?
   - Did you make your goal with two hoola-hoops? How?
   - If you made your goal, how did it feel?
   - If you did not make your goal, what could you do differently next time?

SUMMARY: Remind students that they have to be organized to achieve their goals.

ACTIVITY 4.10: Nothing is Impossible

OBJECTIVE: Students will learn that nothing is impossible when a goal is important to them.

MATERIALS: Construction Paper, Various Art Supplies , Permanent Markers
Optional: White File Folder Labels

PROCEDURES:

1. Write the following quote on the board. "Impossible isn't a word unless you give up," by Mary-Taylor Zorn. Ask students what they think it means. (It means that the word "Impossible" wouldn't exist if you didn't give up. People wouldn't achieve their goals if they gave up).

2. Ask students what would happen if people gave up when their goals became too hard. Discuss the following people in history by asking the students what would have happened if they gave up.

   • Thomas Edison – Teachers told him he was too stupid to learn anything. He was fired from his first two jobs for not being productive. He also failed 1000 times before inventing the light bulb.

   • Walt Disney – He was fired as a newspaper editor because he did not have good ideas or an imagination.

   • Albert Einstein – He did not speak until the age of four and he couldn't read until he was seven. He did not get accepted into the Polytechnic School. He later won the Nobel Prize for changing the world of physics.

   • Oprah Winfrey – She was fired as a TV reporter because she was told she was unfit for TV.

   • J.K. Rowling – Five years before she became one of the richest women in world after publishing her famous Harry Potter series, she was on welfare.

3. Tell students that they are going to make a "Nothing is Impossible Wall" full of goals.

4. Distribute construction paper to each student and various art supplies. Have students trace their hand and part of their arm on the construction paper. Have them decorate their arm and then cut it out.

5. Have the students write one goal on their paper arm somewhere with a permanent marker. (You can also use a file folder label). Make sure they write the number one to signify the first goal they are working on. For next month or quarter, have the students add another goal by writing it on their paper arm or on a file folder label to stick on their paper arm.

6. Have students share their goal with the class.

7. Teacher preparation: On a blank wall put die cut letters that spell out "Nothing is Impossible!" Tape the students' arms on the wall like they are reaching up to the sky.

SUMMARY: Remind the students, that impossible is not a word unless you give up. Many people would not be where they are today if they gave up.

Pay Attention

Overview: Paying attention not only involves listening, but it also involves keeping your eyes on the speaker and actively thinking about what you are hearing. When students are reading, they also need to PAY ATTENTION by thinking about what they read. Paying attention is an important skill for students to learn and often one that is very difficult. In this section, students will learn to practice paying attention in various activities.

PAY ATTENTION Contents:

PAY ATTENTION Parent Letter (Included on CD)

Core Lesson 5 • P- PAY ATTENTION

Activity 5.1 • Bobby Rite Story

Activity 5.2 • The Repeat Game

Activity 5.3 • Name that Object

Activity 5.4 • A Boy Named Jack

Activity 5.5 • Color Magic

Activity 5.6 • Which One?

Activity 5.7 • Study Skills Concentration Game

Activity 5.8 • I Have it!

Activity 5.9 • Pass the Picture

Activity 5.10 • Add On

CORE LESSON 5: "P" – Pay Attention

OBJECTIVE: Students will learn the importance of PAYING ATTENTION in school.

MATERIALS: None

PROCEDURES:

1. Draw the steps on the board like picture A below. Review letters "S," "T," and "E" by asking students what they remember about each letter and why they are important study habits.

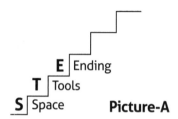

Picture-A

2. Introduce the letter "P" by writing the letter "P" on the next step and the words PAY ATTENTION by it like picture B below. Ask students what it means to PAY ATTENTION. It is when you think about or have interest in something you are listening to or watching.

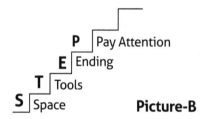

Picture-B

3. Tell students that by tricking their brain it can help them to PAY ATTENTION. Tell students that when their eyes look at something in the classroom, it will tell their brain what to think about. Say to the students, "The teacher may be talking about science, but if I am looking at the globe in the corner, my brain may start to think about the globe. That may then cause me to think about a trip I want to take. Five minutes have now gone by and I don't know what the teacher said."

4. Tell the students that by keeping their eyes on the teacher, even if it is difficult, it will help them to trick their brain and PAY ATTENTION to what the teacher is doing or saying.

5. Role Play: Have a student come up and tell you about a favorite vacation. The first time he/she is talking look around the room, yawning, look at your watch, etc. Have the student repeat what he/she just said only this time PAY ATTENTION by looking at the student, nodding, etc.

CORE LESSON 5: "P" – Pay Attention

CONTINUED...

6. Ask the class the following questions:
   - Which time did I PAY ATTENTION to what you were saying? (The second time)
   - What was different between the two role plays?
   - What would happen if the teacher was talking about science, but you were not PAYING ATTENTION like in the first role play?

7. Discuss how to PAY ATTENTION by modeling the following:
   The 3 "L's" –
   - Look at the speaker
   - Lean in
   - Listen by nodding or asking questions

8. Have each student find a partner. Have one student talk about a favorite birthday, vacation, etc. while the other person practices not PAYING ATTENTION and then PAYING ATTENTION. Have the students then switch roles.

SUMMARY: Remind students that PAYING ATTENTION is more than just listening; it is keeping your eyes on the teacher, sitting up, leaning forward, and nodding.

ACTIVITY 5.1: Bobby Rite Story

OBJECTIVE: Students will learn to PAY ATTENTION by listening to the story and carrying out a given task.

MATERIALS: Bobby Rite Story, One small object per student (I use erasers, but coins or buttons work well too.)

PROCEDURES:

1. Have the students get into a circle. Distribute the small objects to each student.

2. Tell the students that you are going to read a story out loud to them. Every time they hear the word right (spelled many different ways) they are to pass the object to the person on their right. When they hear the word left, they are to pass it to the person on the left.

3. Read the Bobby Rite Story. After you have finished, ask the students what was easy or difficult about the activity. Ask them why it was important to PAY ATTENTION to the directions.

4. Now ask the students what they remember about the story by asking the following questions:

   • By which ear did Bobby Rite's gum get stuck? (Right)
   • What did Bobby Rite run back to get in the morning? (His science project)
   • Where did he leave it at home? (Front hallway table)
   • What side of the bus did Bobby Rite sit? (Left)
   • What was Bobby Rite's friend's name? (Jimmy)
   • Why did the water spill on his lap? (He left the lid off)
   • What did Bobby Rite leave a home? (His math homework)
   • Where did he forget to put it? (In his homework folder)
   • What made him smile at the end of the story? (His mom brought him cupcakes)

5. Ask the students how difficult it was for them to listen for the words "right and left," move the object, and then PAY ATTENTION to the details of the story. Tell the students that sometimes we make errors or miss details when we try to PAY ATTENTION to too many things at once.

SUMMARY: Remind the students that to be most effective, it is best to PAY ATTENTION to one task at a time.

Bobby Rite Story

{ WRITTEN BY BOB ZORN }

Bobby <u>Rite</u> woke up for school one morning, stretched, and ran his <u>left</u> hand through his hair. "What is this!" he exclaimed, as he felt a sticky wad of something on the <u>right</u> side of the head. He remembered he went to bed with chewing gum in his mouth and when he rolled over onto his <u>right</u> side during the night the gum fell out of his mouth and got stuck in his hair near his <u>right</u> ear. To get it out, his mom took her <u>right</u> handed scissors and cut out what was <u>left</u> of the gum in his hair. She then threw it <u>right</u> in the trash can. Bobby <u>Rite</u> looked in the mirror. "Argg! There's nothing <u>left</u> of my hair!" he yelled. "Why did I fall asleep with gum <u>left</u> in my mouth?" he said.

Already running late for school, Bobby <u>Rite</u> ran <u>right</u> to the bus stop when he realized he <u>left</u> his science project on the table <u>right</u> in the front hallway. He quickly ran <u>right</u> back home rushing <u>right</u> through the door when he saw his mom holding it <u>right</u> in her hands waiting for him.

Making it on to the bus without a minute <u>left</u> to spare, Bobby <u>Rite</u> sat in his usual seat on the <u>left</u> side of the bus with his best friend Jimmy <u>right</u> beside him. Jimmy took one look at Bobby <u>Rite</u> and said, "What happened to your hair? There's nothing <u>left</u> on the <u>right</u> side of your head." All Bobby <u>Rite</u> could say was, "Gum! I <u>left</u> gum in my mouth last night."

As the bus driver took a sharp <u>left</u> into the school, Bobby <u>Rite</u> fell to the <u>right</u> and his science project full of water spilled all over his lap. Jimmy, trying hard not to laugh said, "I think you <u>left</u> the lid off your project." All Bobby <u>Rite</u> could say was, "You got that <u>right</u>!"

"What else can go wrong?" Bobby <u>Rite</u> thought as he walked into the school and turned <u>right</u> into Ms. Smith's classroom. As soon as he got into class he realized that he <u>left</u> his math homework on his desk <u>right</u> in his room. "Why didn't I put it in my homework folder on the <u>right</u> side?" he said to himself. "Why me?" Bobby <u>Rite</u> said as he sat <u>right</u> down at his desk.

Just then the loud speaker buzzed into Ms. Smith's room asking Bobby <u>Rite</u> to come <u>right</u> down to the office. "Now what?" he thought. But as he turned <u>right</u> into the office he saw his mom holding cupcakes <u>right</u> in her hands. "You seemed so sad when you <u>left</u> this morning that I thought cupcakes would make things <u>right</u> again." she said. Bobby <u>Rite</u> hugged his mom and took the cupcakes <u>right</u> from her and <u>left</u> for class with a big smile on his face. "It is a mighty <u>right</u> fine day today."

ACTIVITY 5.2: The Repeat Game

OBJECTIVE: Students will learn to PAY ATTENTION by repeating the words in a sentence several times.

MATERIALS: None

PROCEDURES:

1. Have student form a circle in the classroom. Tell the students that they are going to play a game where they will repeat the words of a sentence several times.

2. One person will say the first word from the sentence; the next person in the circle will say the second word from the sentence, and so on.

3. Once you get to the end of the sentence, the words in the sentence are repeated: 2x, 3x, 4x, and then 5x.

4. The sentence is: One dog ate three bones. Yum! Yum!
   If there are 25 students in the class, each one would say the following around the circle:
   - Student 1 says, "One"
   - Student 2 says, "Dog"
   - Student 3 says, "Ate"
   - Student 4 says, "Three"
   - Student 5 says, "Bones"
   - Student 6 says, "Yum"
   - Student 7 says, "Yum."

   Now the students say each word twice.
   - Student 8 says, "One"
   - Student 9 says, "One"
   - Student 10 says, "Dog"
   - Student 11 says, "Dog"
   - Student 12 says, "Ate"
   - Student 13 says, "Ate"
   - Student 14 says, "Three"
   - Student 15 says, "Three"
   - Student 16 says, "Bones"
   - Student 17 says, "Bones"
   - Student 18 says, "Yum"
   - Student 19 says, "Yum"
   - Student 20 says, "Yum"
   - Student 21 says, "Yum."

ACTIVITY 5.2: The Repeat Game

CONTINUED...

Now the students say each word three times.
- Student 22 says, "One"
- Student 23 says, "One"
- Student 24 says, "One"
- Student 25 says, "Dog"
- Student 1 says, "Dog."
- Student 2 says, "Dog"

5. Students will continue with the pattern around the circle. If someone says the wrong word, the class starts again from the beginning with that student saying the first word. You can also tie in goal setting by reviewing the letter "E" for ENDING. Students can set a goal for how far they can get. Make sure you talk about how we treat each other, especially if someone says the wrong word and the class needs to start over.

6. Ask students the following questions:
- What was difficult about this game?
- How was PAYING ATTENTION important during this game?
- Was there something that made the game easier?

SUMMARY: Remind students that when PAYING ATTENTION in class it is important to think about what is being said.

ACTIVITY 5.3: Name that Object

OBJECTIVE: Students will learn to PAY ATTENTION by naming various objects from memory.

MATERIALS: Name that Object Power Point on CD and Name that Object Worksheet (one for each student)

PROCEDURES:

1. Distribute Name that Object Worksheet to each student.

2. Tell the students that you are going to show them a group of pictures on a Power Point slide. Tell them that they will only have a certain number of seconds to see it before it disappears.

3. Tell the students that they will then write down as many of the objects on their worksheet that they can remember when the time is up. Discuss how the students did after each one and the importance of PAYING ATTENTION during this activity.

4. Go through the Power Point slides.

SUMMARY: Remind the students that PAYING ATTENTION not only involves listening, but it also involves actively looking at what they are learning.

Name that Object Worksheet

DIRECTIONS: Write down as many objects that you see from the picture shown on the Power Point slide.

THREE OBJECTS:

1. _____ _____ _____
2. _____ _____ _____

FOUR OBJECTS:

3. _____ _____
   _____ _____
4. _____ _____
   _____ _____

FIVE OBJECTS:

5. _____ _____ _____
   _____ _____
6. _____ _____ _____
   _____ _____

MULTIPLE OBJECTS:

1. _____ 7. _____ 13. _____
2. _____ 8. _____ 14. _____
3. _____ 9. _____ 15. _____
4. _____ 10. _____ 16. _____
5. _____ 11. _____ 17. _____
6. _____ 12. _____ 18. _____

MULTIPLE OBJECTS:

1. _____ 7. _____ 13. _____
2. _____ 8. _____ 14. _____
3. _____ 9. _____ 15. _____
4. _____ 10. _____ 16. _____
5. _____ 11. _____ 17. _____
6. _____ 12. _____ 18. _____

ACTIVITY 5.4: A Boy Named Jack

OBJECTIVE: Students will learn to PAY ATTENTION by naming various objects from memory

MATERIALS: White drawing paper, Crayons, markers, or colored pencils

PROCEDURES:

1. Preparation: Make a sample picture of Jack to show the students after they have done the activity.

2. Distribute paper and art supplies to students.

3. Tell the students that you are going to read a poem to them just once. They are then going to draw a picture of what they hear. Remind the students that they must PAY ATTENTION to the poem in order to draw the correct picture with the correct details.

4. Read the poem, "A Boy Named Jack." Have students draw a picture of Jack.

A BOY NAMED JACK
His head was as flat as a tack.
He wore an orange shirt that had green polka dots too.
And his pants were a very bright, royal blue.

His ears stuck out from his short brown hair.
And his feet were so big that people often stared.
Jack didn't care though about what the people said.
He just smiled and tipped his hat that was red.

The town folk grew to love Jack, as colorful as he looked.
That they even wrote a story about him and put him in a book.

5. Show the students the sample picture you made. Have students share their version of what Jack looks like. Tell the students that it is important to PAY ATTENTION to details when listening as well as reading. Tell the students that it can also help to picture what is being said or what they read in their mind.

VARIATION: After the students draw the first picture, read the story a couple more times. Discuss the importance of PAYING ATTENTION to details that were missed.

SUMMARY: Remind the students that it is important to PAY ATTENTION to details when listening and reading.

ACTIVITY 5.5: Color Magic Game

OBJECTIVE: Students will learn how to PAY ATTENTION for details and cues to discover the secret to how a game is played.

MATERIALS: None

PROCEDURES:

1. Preparation:
   - Select one student to help you with this activity.
   - Meet with this student in private before the activity begins to tell him/her how the game is played.
   - Tell the student that a random object will be picked in the room by the other students while he/she is out of the room. When the student comes back in the room, he/she will be able to guess what the object is.
   - Tell the student that the color BLUE is the magic color (you can pick any color). Once the object is chosen by the class you will bring the student back in the room.
   - You will name various objects in the room by saying their color first. For example, you would say, "Is it the green book?" The student would say, "No." "Is it the red sweater?" the student would say, "No." Is it the black trash can?" The student would say, "No."
   - When you name something that is BLUE ("Is it the BLUE marker?"), that is the clue for the student to know that the very next object is the one chosen by the class.

2. Ask the students that you need a volunteer to help you with this activity. Select the student who you met with prior to the game.

3. Tell the class that the volunteer is going to go outside the classroom. When the student is gone, have someone name an object in the room. (example: the pink eraser)

4. Bring the student back in the room and start naming objects from around the room as mentioned above.

5. Once you name something BLUE, the student will know that the next object is the one that the class picked. For example: "Is it the BLUE folder?" The student will say "No." "Is it the pink eraser?" The student will say, "Yes."

6. At this time, the class will wonder how the student guessed the object. They may say that the student could hear through the door. If this is the case, you can send another student outside with the student to make sure he/she is not listening. This makes it even more fun.

7. Tell the students that they are to PAY ATTENTION by trying to figure out how the student is able to guess the object.

8. Continue for several more rounds. After each round ask the students if they figured it out by sharing their guess out loud or in your ear if you don't want others to know.

9. Once everyone knows how the game is played ask students how they figured it out. Ask them why it was important to PAY ATTENTION to details in this game.

SUMMARY: Remind the students that it is important to PAY ATTENTION to details when listening and reading.

ACTIVITY 5.6: Which One?

OBJECTIVE: Students will learn to PAY ATTENTION by following directions given to them.

MATERIALS: Reproducible – Which One? (Copied and cut apart)

PROCEDURES:

1. Have students stand up near their desks.

2. Tell the students that you are going to read four directions to them and then tell them to do number one, two, three, or four.

3. Tell the students that they must PAY ATTENTION to the four directions read out loud so they will know which one to do.

4. Read one of the Which One? cards and pick number 1-4 for the student to do. Continue with the other cards.

5. After reading the cards ask the students the following questions:

   - What was difficult about this activity?
   - Did you find yourself getting better with each round?
   - How did you PAY ATTENTION?
   - How does this activity relate to PAYING ATTENTION to the teacher?

SUMMARY: Tell the students that to PAY ATTENTION they must listen to and follow directions.

Which One? Worksheet

1. Clap your hands two times
2. Hop on one foot
3. Turn around twice
4. Touch your nose

---

1. Do four jumping jacks
2. Touch your toes
3. Sit down in your chair
4. Fold your arms

---

1. Put your hands on your head
2. Clap your hands four times
3. Snap your fingers
4. Turn around three times

---

1. Sing Twinkle, Twinkle Little Star
2. Shake hands with a friend
3. Touch your knees
4. Stomp your feet

---

1. Put your hands on your hips
2. Close your eyes
3. Reach for the sky
4. Wave to the teacher

---

1. Sing Happy Birthday to yourself
2. Jog in place
3. Sit on the ground
4. Hop on your left foot

---

1. Clap five times
2. Hop like a frog
3. Say hello to someone
4. Walk around your desk

---

1. Snap your fingers ten times
2. Rub your tummy
3. Touch your shoulders
4. Stand on your tip toes

Which One? Worksheet

1. Do ten jumping jacks
2. Write your name in the air
3. Touch the ground
4. Pat your knees five times

1. Wiggle your fingers
2. Touch your nose
3. Hop on your right foot
4. Sing the alphabet

1. Stomp your feet
2. Wiggle your ears
3. Nod your head up and down
4. Walk around the room

1. Put your hands in the air
2. Clap once then snap your fingers twice
3. Jog in place
4. Wave at four friends

1. Touch your left elbow with your right hand
2. Walk around your desk
3. Jump seven times
4. Touch your head

1. Touch your nose ten times
2. Put your right foot over your left foot
3. Clap your hands six times
4. Shake hands with a friend

1. Snap your fingers five times
2. Hop up and down
3. Touch your toes
4. Sing the alphabet

1. Put your hands on your head
2. Turn around ten times
3. Hop like a frog
4. Sit in your chair

ACTIVITY 5.7: Study Skills Concentration Game

OBJECTIVE: Students will practice PAYING ATTENTION by memorizing and matching pictures that represent tools used by students.

MATERIALS: Reproducible – Study Skills Concentration Cards (one set for each group of 4-5 students)

PROCEDURES:

1. Divide the class into groups of 4-5 students.

2. Tell the students that they are going to play a matching game called study skills concentration.

3. Distribute the Study Skills Concentration sets to each group.

4. Tell students to put the cards in front of them upside down and mixed up. Have the student whose birthday is closest to today begin by turning over two cards. If the cards are a match, have the student keep the cards in front of him/her. Then continue to the next student even if the student found a match.

5. Ask students why it is important to PAY ATTENTION during this game. They need to PAY ATTENTION so they will see what cards are being turned over and where they are located.

6. Ask students how this relates to PAYING ATTENTION in school.

7. Continue play until all the matches are found.

8. Play as many rounds as time allows.

SUMMARY: Remind students that PAYING ATTENTION in school is a lot like playing this game. They need to keep their eyes on the teacher and listen so they do not miss anything.

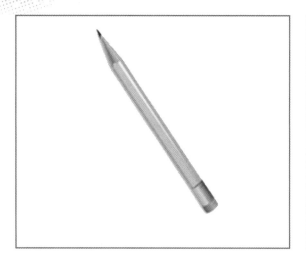

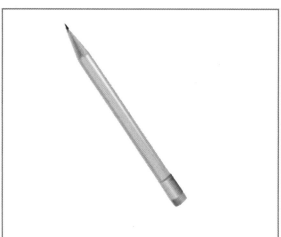

crayons

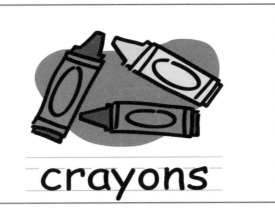

crayons

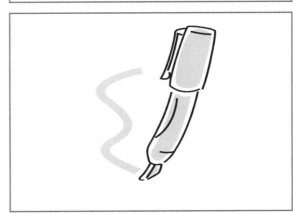

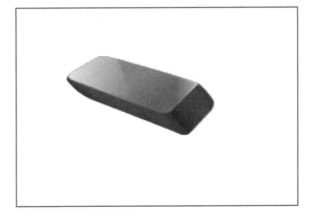

Study Skills Concentration Cards

 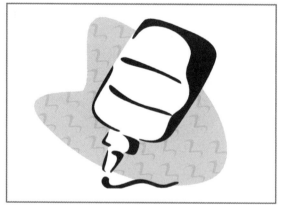

Study Skills Concentration Cards

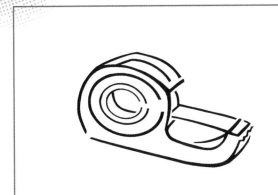 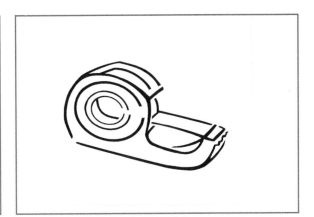

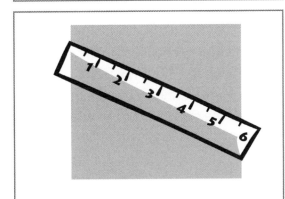 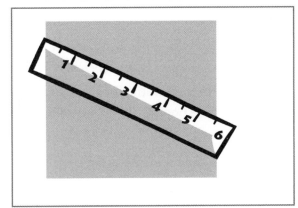

ACTIVITY 5.8: I Have It!

OBJECTIVE: Students will learn to PAY ATTENTION to the objects written on the cards and respond when their object is named.

MATERIALS: Reproducible – I Have It! Cards (copied on cardstock, laminated, and cut apart)

PROCEDURES:

1. Remind students what it means to PAY ATTENTION. It means to think about what you are listening to or watching.

2. Tell students that they are going to practice PAYING ATTENTION today.

3. Distribute I Have It! cards to each student. (Some students may have more than one card.)

4. Tell the students that the person who has the card with the "School Bus" in the corner will begin the game by saying, "I have the pencil. Who has the book bag?" (This is written and shown on the card). The student that has the card with the book bag will say, "I have the book bag. Who has the agenda book?" The game will continue until all the cards have been called out and the last person says, "Now I can start my homework!"

5. Ask students the following questions:
   • Why did everyone need to PAY ATTENTION during the game?
   • What happens when someone does not PAY ATTENTION during this activity?
   • How does this activity relate to PAYING ATTENTION during class?

SUMMARY: Remind the students that by keeping their eyes on the teacher and thinking about what the teacher is saying will help them to PAY ATTENTION in school.

I have the Pencil.

Who has the Book Bag?

I have the Book Bag.

Who has the Agenda Book?

I have the Agenda Book.

Who has the Crayons?

crayons

I have the Crayons.

crayons

Who has the Homework Folder?

I have the Homework Folder.

Who has the Eraser?

I have the Eraser.

Who has the Colored Pencils?

I have the Colored Pencils.

Who has the Scissors?

I have the Scissors.

Who has the Glue?

I have the Glue.

Who has the Paper?

I have the Paper.

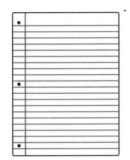

Who has the Tape?

I have the Tape.

Who has the Ruler?

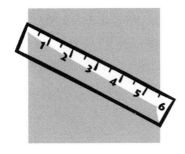

I have the Ruler.

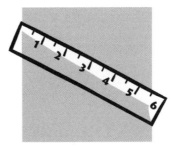

Who has the Toolbox?

I have the Toolbox.

Who has the Books?

I have the Books.

Who has the Highlighter?

I have the Highlighter.

Who has the Markers?

I have the Markers.

Who has the
Construction Paper?

I have the
Construction Paper.

Who has the Pencil
Sharpener?

I have the Pencil
Sharpener.

Who has the Desk?

I have the Desk

Who has the Chair?

I have the Chair.

Who has the Flash Cards?

I have the Flash Cards.

Who has the Composition Book?

I have the Composition Book.

Who has the Pens?

I have the Pens?

Who has the Index Cards?

I have the Index Cards.

Who has the Protractor?

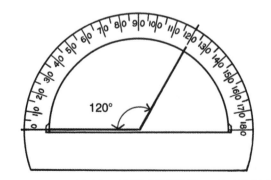

I Have It! Cards

I have the Protractor.

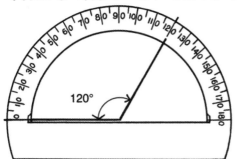

120°

Who has the Binder?

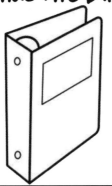

I have the Binder.

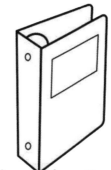

Who has the Computer?

I have the Computer.

Who has the Water Bottle?

I have the Water Bottle.

Now I can start my Homework!

ACTIVITY 5.9: Pass the Picture

OBJECTIVE: Students will learn to PAY ATTENTION to kinesthetic cues to guess the object they feel.

MATERIALS: Reproducible – Picture Cards cut apart, Dry erase boards and markers or paper and a pencil for each group

PROCEDURES:

1. Divide the class in groups of 4-5 students.

2. Have each group stand in a line so that one student is facing the back of another student.

3. Tell the students that you are going to show the last person in each line a picture. They are then going to draw the picture on the back of the person in front of them only using their finger. Each person in line will then draw what they feel on their back onto the back of the next person in line. They can draw it more than once if need be.

4. The last person in line will draw the picture they felt on either a Dry Erase board or a piece of paper and write down the name of the object. For example, if the picture drawn is a snowman, the last person will actually draw a snowman and write down the word snowman.

5. Once everyone has finished, check and see how many groups named the object correctly. Continue by having everyone move up so there is a new person naming the picture. (It is funny to see what they name as their objects).

6. After everyone has had a turn naming the picture, ask the students the following questions:
   - What was difficult about this activity?
   - What was easy about this activity?
   - How did PAYING ATTENTION play a part in this activity?
   - What would have happened if you were the one who did not PAY ATTENTION to what was drawn on your back?
   - Why is it important to PAY ATTENTION to the way something is taught?

SUMMARY: Remind students that it is important to PAY ATTENTION to details so they do not miss anything.

Snowman

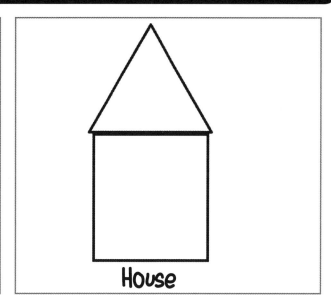
House

Star

Heart

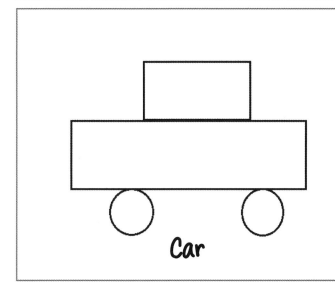
Car

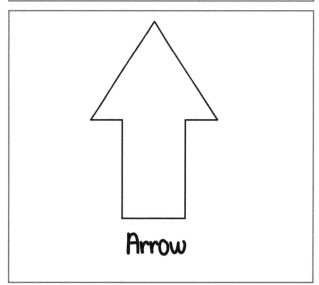
Arrow

ACTIVITY 5.10: Add On

OBJECTIVE: Students will learn to PAY ATTENTION to visual cues given by their peers so they can repeat them.

MATERIALS: None

PROCEDURES:

1. Divide the class into groups of 8-12 students. There can be less for small groups.
2. Have the students stand in a circle. Tell the students that they are going to make an action such as clap their hands, stomp their feet, turn around, etc.
3. One student in the circle will begin with an action. Play will continue clockwise with the next student repeating what the first student did and then adding on to the game. For example, student #1 may clap his/her hand two times. Student #2 will clap his/her hands two times and then turn around. Student #3 will clap his/her hands two times, turn around, and then wave to a friend, etc.
4. If a student does not do the sequence correctly, you can decide on the following options:

   • The game can start over with new actions. They would need to start from where they left off.
   • The group can help the student by telling him/her the action that comes next.
   • This can also be a goal setting activity to tie in "Ending" and "Pay Attention" where the group continues to set new goals.
5. Discuss the importance of PAYING ATTENTION during this activity. Ask students what strategies they used to help them PAY ATTENTION.

SUMMARY: Remind students that to PAY ATTENTION, they must also concentrate on what they are doing or listening to at all times.

Understand Directions

Overview: Understanding directions is an important habit for students to learn in school. Every day teachers give students oral directions for various tasks which they are expected to follow. On assignments students must also read the written directions in order to do the assignment correctly. What often happens is that students think they know what to do only to find out later that it was wrong. In this section students will learn to follow oral and written directions through various activities.

UNDERSTAND DIRECTIONS Contents:

UNDERSTAND DIRECTIONS Parent Letter (Included on CD)

Core Lesson 6 • U – UNDERSTAND DIRECTIONS

Written Directions

Activity 6.1 • What's the Answer?

Activity 6.2 • A Beautiful Day!

Activity 6.3 • Create a Picture

Activity 6.4 • Written Directions Test

Activity 6.5 • Create Your Shape

Oral Directions

Activity 6.6 • Picture Perfect

Activity 6.7 • Do as I say...Do as I do

Activity 6.8 • Break the Code

Activity 6.9 • The Human Pretzel

Activity 6.10 • Where Am I?

Optional Activity 6.11 • Bop-It

CORE LESSON 6: "U" – Understand Directions

OBJECTIVE: Students will learn the importance of understanding written and oral directions in school.

MATERIALS: None

PROCEDURES:

1. Draw the steps on the board like picture A below. Review letters "S," "T," "E," and "P" by asking students what they remember about each letter and why they are important study habits.

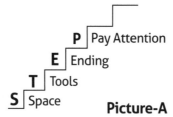

Picture-A

2. Introduce the letter "U" by writing the letter "U" on the next step and the words UNDERSTAND DIRECTIONS by it like picture B below. Ask students what it means to UNDERSTAND DIRECTIONS.

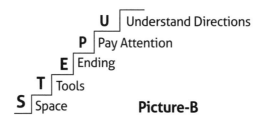

Picture-B

3. Ask students what are the two kinds of directions they follow at school. They are oral and written directions.

4. Ask students what part of their body they use for oral directions. (Ears) When teachers give students directions they must listen to what is said and then do the task. Ask students why it is important to follow oral directions at school.

5. Ask students what part of their body they use for written directions. (Eyes) Ask students how many times they should read the directions. Discuss when students get an assignment with written directions they need to read the directions at least 2-3 times before doing anything. Ask the students if they have ever turned an assignment in to only have the teacher say, "Go back and read the directions." This is because students think they know what to do.

6. Tell students that another mistake students make with written directions is not doing all of what is asked. Explain that some directions may have two parts. For example, it may say to list four examples of the Industrial Revolution and why they had an impact on the United States. Students will list the examples, but forget to explain the impact. One way to see how well they followed written directions is to look at their graded work that goes home.

SUMMARY: Remind students that following directions is an important habit. Many students make careless errors because they didn't follow the directions. They knew the material, but they received a lower grade due to not following the directions.

ACTIVITY 6.1: What's the Answer?

OBJECTIVE: Students will learn to follow written directions by reading the instructions carefully.

MATERIALS: What's the Answer? Worksheet (one for each student), Pencils

PROCEDURES:

1. Distribute What's the Answer? Worksheet to students.

2. Tell students that they have five minutes to complete as many problems that they can according to the directions.

3. Say, "Stop" when time is up. Tell the students that you are going to read the answers to the problems in both sections. Ask students to raise their hand if they were able to get all of them correct.

4. At this time some of the students may be wondering why they got them wrong. Ask a student to read the written directions in the first section. Tell the students that the directions say to change each sign to another and then compute the problem.

5. Ask a student to read the directions in the second section. The directions say to compute the problem and then add two to get the answer.

6. Ask students why it is important to read the directions. Discuss answers. Tell the students that if they turned this paper in to their teacher, they would have received a zero for their grade.

SUMMARY: Remind students that even when they think they know what to do, it is still important to read the directions to make sure they are following the instructions correctly.

NAME _____

DIRECTIONS: For each of the following problems, when you see a multiplication sign, change it to a subtraction sign. When you see an addition sign, change it to a multiplication sign. And when you see a subtraction sign, change it to an addition sign. Then compute the problem.

1. $7 \times 2 =$ _____

2. $41 - 11 =$ _____

3. $4 + 30 =$ _____

4. $7 \times 7 =$ _____

5. $19 - 5 =$ _____

6. $18 + 4 =$ _____

7. $12 \times 3 =$ _____

8. $36 - 2 =$ _____

9. $20 + 6 =$ _____

10. $10 \times 9 =$ _____

DIRECTIONS: Compute the following problems and then add 2 to get the answer.

1. $16 + 11 =$ _____

2. $10 \times 6 =$ _____

3. $74 - 18 =$ _____

4. $48 + 10 =$ _____

5. $4 \times 11 =$ _____

6. $88 - 10 =$ _____

7. $97 + 14 =$ _____

8. $5 \times 5 =$ _____

9. $37 - 4 =$ _____

10. $34 + 5 =$ _____

What's the Answer? Answer Key

DIRECTIONS: For each of the following problems, when you see a multiplication sign, change it to a subtraction sign. When you see an addition sign, change it to a multiplication sign. And when you see a subtraction sign, change it to an addition sign. Then compute the problem.

1. $7 \times 2 = 5$

2. $41 - 11 = 52$

3. $4 + 30 = 120$

4. $7 \times 7 = 0$

5. $19 - 5 = 24$

6. $18 + 4 = 72$

7. $12 \times 3 = 9$

8. $36 - 2 = 38$

9. $20 + 6 = 120$

10. $10 \times 9 = 1$

DIRECTIONS: Compute the following problems and then add 2 to get the answer.

1. $16 + 11 = 29$

2. $10 \times 6 = 62$

3. $74 - 18 = 58$

4. $48 + 10 = 60$

5. $4 \times 11 = 46$

6. $88 - 10 = 80$

7. $97 + 14 = 113$

8. $5 \times 5 = 27$

9. $37 - 4 = 35$

10. $34 + 5 = 41$

ACTIVITY 6.2: A Beautiful Day!

OBJECTIVE: Students will follow the written directions to create a picture by using the details from a story.

MATERIALS: A Beautiful Day (one for each student), Art Supplies (crayons, markers, or colored pencils)

PROCEDURES:

1. Distribute A Beautiful Day sheet and art supplies to each student.

2. Tell the students that they are to read the story first before doing anything and then create a picture in the box using the details from the story.

3. After the students have finished drawing their pictures, have them compare what they did with the other students. Were the pictures similar or different?

4. Ask them what was easy or difficult about this activity. Ask the students if they started drawing something before they read the whole story. For example, ask the students if they started coloring the squirrels gray before they learned that they were supposed to be black or did they also start coloring the house a certain color before they read what color it should be.

5. Ask the students what happens when they start to do an assignment without reading all the directions. Often they did the assignment wrong and will have to re-do it.

SUMMARY: Remind the students that even when they think they know what to do, it is important to read all the directions.

A Beautiful Day!

DIRECTIONS: Draw a picture by using the details in the story below.

It is a beautiful day! The yellow sun has orange rays streaming out of it on the top left side of the blue sky. There is a house on the far right with a purple door and two windows on each side. I see a little girl with orange pig tails peeping out of the right window looking at the black and white dog trying to catch the squirrels. A big oak tree grows tall by the left side of the house. It has big green leaves that reach into the blue sky. Two black squirrels tease the dog while chasing each other up and down the trunk of the brown and black tree. The green grass grows all around the red house and the tree, and I can almost smell the bouquet of pink flowers growing to the left of the tree. Ahhhh! What a beautiful day!

ACTIVITY 6.3: Create a Picture

OBJECTIVE: Students will learn to follow written directions to create a picture.

MATERIALS: Create a Picture by Annlen Zorn (one for each student), Art Supplies (crayons, markers, or colored pencils)

PROCEDURES:

1. Distribute Make a Picture sheet and art supplies to all students.

2. Tell the students that they must use their art supplies to follow the written directions on their sheet to create a picture. Go over the Color Key with the students.

3. After they have finished ask the students what was difficult about this activity.

4. Discuss that not only did they have to follow the written directions, but they also had to pay attention to each box to make sure they colored the right part the right way.

SUMMARY: Discuss that it is important to read or look at written directions more than once to make sure they are doing what the directions say.

Create a Picture

1	2	3	4	5
6	7	8	9	10
11	12	13	14	15
16	17	18	19	20

Directions: Color each box according to the key and shape below.

Y = Yellow, R = Red, O = Orange, P = Purple, B = Blue, G = Green

17
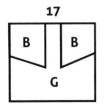

4
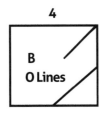

16, 18, 19, 20
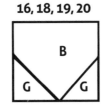

7
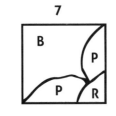

10
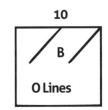

5
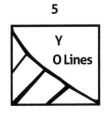

8
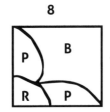

12
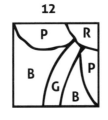

13
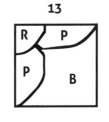

1, 2, 3, 6, 9, 11, 14, 15
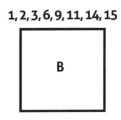

ACTIVITY 6.4: Written Directions Test

OBJECTIVE: Students will learn to follow the written directions before starting an activity.

MATERIALS: Getting to Know You Worksheet (one for each student), Pencils

PROCEDURES:

1. Distribute the Getting to Know You worksheet to each student upside down.

2. Tell the students that you want to get to know them a little bit better. Tell them to read the directions before starting and when they are finished they can turn their paper over and draw a picture until the others are finished.

3. The directions say to only do number two and eight. Watch and see how many students read the directions first or start completing the worksheet right away. You will be surprised at how many students will start answering the questions.

4. When everyone is finished, have a student read the directions out loud. Discuss what happens when students do not follow the written directions. Tell the students that before they started you reminded them to read the directions and if this was for a grade, many students would receive a zero.

5. After discussing the importance of following written directions, have the students finish the questions. Have the students share some of the answers with the class. Then collect these to look back on throughout the school year.

SUMMARY: Remind the students that even if they think they know what to do it is important to first read all the written directions.

Getting to Know You Worksheet

DIRECTIONS: Below are several getting to know you questions. Only answer numbers two and eight. When you are finished turn your paper over and draw a picture.

1. What is your name?

_____

2. What is your favorite ice-cream flavor?

_____

3. What is your favorite school subject?

_____

4. Do you play any sports? If so which one(s)?

_____

5. What is your favorite activity to do?

_____

6. Who is your favorite college football team?

_____

7. Where would you like to go on vacation?

_____

8. Do you have any pets? If so which ones?

_____

9. How many brothers and sisters do you have?

_____

10. What do you want to do as a career?

_____

ACTIVITY 6.5: Create Your Shape

OBJECTIVE: Students will follow the written directions to create unique shapes.

MATERIALS: Create Your Shape (one for each student), Art Supplies (crayons, markers, or colored pencils)

PROCEDURES:

1. Preparation: Make a sample Create Your Shape sheet to show students once they finish the activity.

2. Ask students to raise their hand if they have ever had an assignment returned to them because they did not follow the written directions. Ask them what happens when they do not follow the written directions on an assignment.

3. Distribute Create Your Shape worksheet and art supplies to students. Review with the students how to follow grid lines by looking for where the letter and the number intersect.

4. Have students practice following the written directions by reading the details and completing the shapes. Remind the students that some shape designs are easy and some are more difficult and they must read the directions several times to make sure they are doing the assignment correctly.

5. Show the students your sample sheet when they have finished the activity. Ask the students what was easy about this activity. Ask the students what was difficult about this activity. Ask them how doing this activity can help them to remember to read the directions completely before doing their assignments.

SUMMARY: Remind the students that it is important to PAY ATTENTION to details when reading written directions.

Create Your Shape

DIRECTIONS: Follow the directions below to complete the boxes.

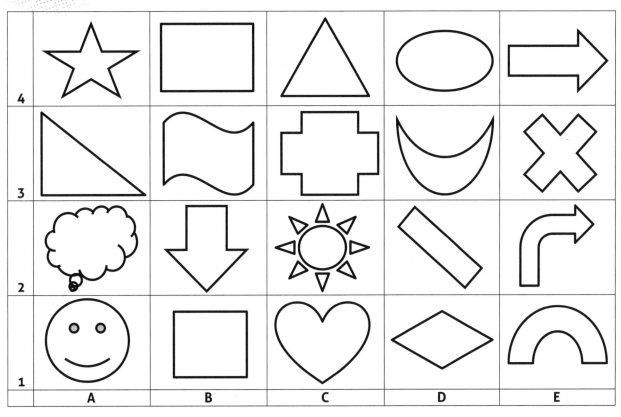

A1: Color the shape purple and add a black mustache.

E4: Draw another shape like this one inside it facing the other way that is blue.

B3: Color the shape red, orange, and red so it looks like stripes.

C2: Color the circle yellow and the triangles orange.

A4: Color the top and bottom two points blue and the two side points red. Color the outside yellow.

D3: Put teeth in this shape.

B2: Draw a yellow star inside this shape.

E1: Color the shape red, orange, yellow, and purple following the same form of the shape.

C4: Divide the shape in half from the top point. Color the left side green and the right side orange.

D1: Color the shape blue and the outside yellow.

A3: Draw a person sliding down the green shape.

B4: Draw two pink flowers with green stems inside the shape.

E3: Color the shape red and the outside black.

C1: Color the shape pink. Draw an arrow through it so it points out the bottom left side of the shape.

D2: Write the word fun in red inside the shape. Color the outside purple.

B1: Draw a brown line from the top left corner to the bottom right corner. Do the same on the other side.

A2: Write, "I can follow directions" in the shape.

C3: Divide the shape in half from the middle left to the middle right. Color the left side red and the right side blue.

E2: Color the shape orange and the outside black.

D4: Draw the same shape as in C1, then color purple inside this shape.

ACTIVITY 6.6: Picture Perfect

OBJECTIVE: Students will learn to draw a picture by following the oral directions.

MATERIALS: Blank paper (one for each student), Art Supplies (crayons, markers, or colored pencils), Sample pictures (black and white or color on flash drive)

PROCEDURES:

1. Distribute paper and art supplies to students. (don't show students the sample page until they finish their drawings)

2. Tell the students that they need to listen carefully to the oral directions in order to draw the correct picture. Have the students put the paper vertically in front of them.

3. Read the following directions twice.

   • Draw a small circle in the middle of the paper. Color it blue.

   • Draw another circle around the first circle. Color it red.

   • Draw another circle around the second circle. Color it purple.

   • Draw a large triangle with the top point touching the bottom of the circle.

   • Put three green squares in the triangle.

   • Draw a rectangle under the bottom triangle. Write your name inside it.

   • Draw a medium sized rectangle touching the left side of the circle. Put a yellow happy face inside the rectangle.

   • Draw a medium sized rectangle touching the right side of the circle. Put an orange sun inside the rectangle.

   • Draw a large triangle with the point touching the top of the circle.

   • Draw five yellow stars inside the top triangle.

   • Draw a pink heart on the line of the top triangle.

4. Now show students the sample picture. Ask the students what was easy or difficult about this activity.

5. Ask the students what happened if parts of their picture looked different from the sample. Tell the students that sometimes what we think we hear is not what was said. Ask students how they can make sure they heard the oral directions correctly. They can repeat what they heard in their head to help them remember.

SUMMARY: Remind the students that to follow oral directions they need to PAY ATTENTION to what is being said by thinking about what was said before doing the task.

Picture Perfect

Your Name

ACTIVITY 6.7: Do as I say...Do as I Do

OBJECTIVE: Students will learn to PAY ATTENTION to auditory and visual directions.

MATERIALS: Do as I say...Do as I do examples

PROCEDURES:

1. This activity takes a little bit of thinking on your part, but the students really enjoy it. Tell the students that they are going to play a game where they will either do what you say or what you do.

2. Have the students do what you say. Always say, "Do as I say" before you ask them what to do. Don't do the action, just say it. Practice the following:

    Say to the students:

    "Do as I say, Look at the ceiling." (Students should be looking up at the ceiling)

    "Do as I say, Clap your hands."

    "Do as I say, Touch your nose."

    "Do as I say, Wave your hands."

3. Have the students do what you do. Always say, "Do as I do" before you do the action. Don't say what you are doing, just do the action.

    Say, "Do as I do." (You clap your hands)

    Say, "Do as I do." (You touch your toes)

    Say, "Do as I do." (You turn around)

    Say, "Do as I do." (You hop on one foot)

4. Tell the students that they had to PAY ATTENTION by using their ears when you said "Do as I say." And they had to use their eyes when you said "Do as I do."

5. Now you are going to combine the two. For example, you may say, "Do as I say, Jump up and down." But at the same time you are clapping your hands. The students need to do what you SAY, not what you DO because you said, "Do as I say." Another example is saying, "Do as I do." You then turn around, but at the same time you say, "Touch your head." The students should be turning around because you said, "Do as I do," even though you said, "Touch your head."

6. Use Do as I say...Do as I do examples by saying either one first and then doing the other. For example, on the first one you can say to the students:

    "Do as I do." (You hop on one foot while saying, "Touch your knees.") The students should be only hopping.

    Or you can say,

    "Do as I say, Touch your knees." (You should be hopping) The students should only be touching their knees.

7. Continue with the rest of the list by saying, "Do as I say or Do as I do."

8. Discussion questions:
   • What was difficult about this game?
   • Did you feel the game became easier as you went along?
   • How did it get easier?
   • Why was it important to PAY ATTENTION during this game?
   • How can this game help you to PAY ATTENTION in the classroom?

SUMMARY: Remind the students that paying attention not only involves using their ears to listen, but their eyes as well

Do as I say...Do as I Do Example Sheet

DIRECTIONS: Say one from the "Do as I Say" side while doing one from the "Do as I Do" side. Do one from the "Do as I Do" side while saying one from the "Do as I say" side. Remember to always say, "Do as I Say" or "Do as I Do" before each game.

DO AS I SAY	DO AS I DO
• Touch your knees	• Hop on one foot
• Look at the ceiling	• Wave your hands
• Turn-around	• Touch your knees
• Wave your hands	• Clap your hands
• Stomp your feet	• Blink your eyes
• Wiggle your ears	• Put your hands on your hips
• Blink your eyes	• Reach for the sky
• Jump up and down	• Look at the ceiling
• Flap your arms	• Touch your toes
• Put your hands on your hips	• Turn-around
• Reach for the sky	• Sit down
• Hop on one foot	• Touch your nose
• Touch your toes	• Flap your arms
• Clap your hands	• Jump up and down
• Sit down	• Wiggle your ears
• Touch your nose	• Stomp your feet

ACTIVITY 6.8: Break the Code

OBJECTIVE: Students will learn to follow oral directions to break the code.

MATERIALS: Break the Code (one for each student), Pencil

PROCEDURES:

1. Review oral directions with the students by asking them what part of their body they use for oral directions. They use their ears to listen and then follow the directions.

2. Distribute Break the Code sheet to students. Tell the students that you are going to give them some oral directions. They must follow these directions to get the correct numbers below in order to break the code. Tell the students that each group of squares is a word.

3. Oral Directions:

- For the first four words, change the number in the box to the number that is two less than what is written. Write that number in the box below it. For example, for the first word ask the students what number is two less than 11. It is nine. Have them write the number nine in the box below number 11. Do the rest the same way.

- For the next two words, change the number in the box to five more than what is written. Write that number in the box below it. (At this time you may see some students erasing because they went ahead and followed the same oral directions as the first four words. Stop and talk about what happens when they do not follow the teacher's oral directions. They will not know what to do or get the assignment wrong.)

- For the last two words, change the number in the box to one less than what is written. Write that number in the box below.

- Once they have followed your oral directions, tell the students to use the code at the bottom of the page to see what the message says.

4. Ask students what it says. (I use my ears to follow oral directions.)

SUMMARY: Remind the students to listen carefully to the oral directions. Tell them to think about what was said in their mind first, and then do the task.

Break the Code

NAME: _____

DIRECTIONS: Follow the oral directions to break the code.

11

23	21	7

15	27

7	3	20	21

15	10

1	10	7	7	10	18

16	19	2	13

5	10	19	6	4	21	10	16	15	20

What does it say? _____

1-A	2-B	3-C	4-D	5-E	6-F	7-G	8-H	9-I	10-J	11-K	12-L	13-M	14-N

15-O	16-P	17-Q	18-R	19-S	20-T	21-U	22-V	23-W	24-X	25-Y	26-Z

ACTIVITY 6.9: The Human Pretzel

OBJECTIVE: Students will learn to follow oral directions to play a game of Human Pretzel.

MATERIALS: The Human Pretzel Directions

PROCEDURES:

1. Have students stand up. Make sure they have a small open space to move around.

2. Tell the students that you are going to give them some oral directions to follow like the game "Simon Says." However, tell them that you will say your name instead. For example, if your name is Ms. Smith, you will say, "Ms. Smith says to hop on one foot."

3. Students will, however, continue to add on the directions until you say, "Ms. Smith says Freeze!" Then the students will return to a standing position to wait for the next set of directions. For example, "Ms. Smith says to touch your nose." "Ms. Smith says to turn around." "Ms. Smith says to pat your head." The students should be doing all three of those oral directions at once until you say, "Ms. Smith says Freeze."

4. If you say, "Ms. Smith says to stomp your feet." "Wiggle your fingers." Everybody who started wiggling their fingers is out and should sit down. The students who followed the oral directions should still be stomping their feet.

5. Use the Human Pretzel Directions sheet for examples. Play as many rounds as you would like until there is a winner or you want everybody to start again. Begin the game.

6. Discussion questions:
  • How did the letter "P" for PAY ATTENTION play into following the oral directions?
  • What was difficult about this activity?
  • Did the game get easier as you went along?
  • How can this activity help you when your teacher gives you oral directions?

SUMMARY: Remind the students that to UNDERSTAND ORAL DIRECTIONS, it is important to PAY ATTENTION by listening and thinking about what was said before doing the task.

The Human Pretzel

DIRECTIONS: Read two to four of the oral directions below that you think the students can do at once. If you want them to follow the oral direction say, "Your Name and the oral direction below." If not, just say the direction. To start over, say "Your Name says, Freeze!" For example, "Ms. Norton says, Freeze!"

EXAMPLES:

- Touch your right elbow to your left knee
- Hop on your left foot
- Jump up and down
- Put your hands on your hips
- Touch your toes
- Touch your right ear with your left hand
- Pat your head
- Rub your tummy
- Turn around
- Touch your nose
- Wiggle your fingers in the air
- Look at the ground
- Stomp your feet
- Stand on your tip toes
- Reach for the ceiling

- Put your left hand on your right shoulder
- Put your right hand on your left shoulder
- Touch the ground
- Touch your left elbow
- Put your nose on your right knee
- Touch your shoulders
- Touch your right elbow
- Clap your hands
- Sit on the ground
- Hop like a frog
- Touch your left elbow to your right knee
- Wave to a friend
- Cluck like a chicken
- Hop on your right foot

ACTIVITY 6.10: Where Am I?

OBJECTIVE: Students will learn to follow oral directions to find a particular location.

MATERIALS: Where Am I? sheet (one for each student), Pencils

PROCEDURES:

1. Distribute Where Am I? sheets to students.

2. Tell the students that you are going to give them some oral directions to follow. They must PAY ATTENTION to what you are saying in order to find the correct location.

3. Remind the students that North is up. South is down. East is right. And West is left. When they find the correct location, have the students write the place down on the line at the bottom of page.

4. Practice round: Tell the students to start at the tennis courts. Travel north to Cherry Street. Turn left at Cherry Street. Turn right on 5th Avenue. Your destination is on the right. Write where they are on line one at the bottom of the sheet. (Answer: Doctor's office)

5. Continue by making up directions to various locations starting from different parts of the city. Have the students then write the locations down on the lines at the bottom of sheet.

6. Ask students what was easy or difficult about this activity. Ask them why paying attention to the oral directions was important. (This was an activity where the students had to pay attention to the directions. It was not an activity that they could do if on their own).

SUMMARY: Remind the students that it is important to PAY ATTENTION when following oral directions so they will know how to locate places on a map.

Where Am I?

NAME: _____

Dentist	Burger Stop	Hospital		Beauty Salon
James Street				
	Pool	Doctor's Offices	**Dog Park**	Football Field
Cherry Street				
			Movie Theater	
Green Street				
	Mexican Restaurant	The Mall		Italian Restaurant
Willow Street				
Drug Store	Grocery Store		Library	School
Oak Street				
		City Hall	Ballet Studio	Tennis Courts
Harper Street				
	Auto Repair			

8th Avenue   6th Avenue   5th Avenue   4th Avenue   2nd Avenue

DIRECTIONS: Write the location according to the oral directions given.

1. _____   6. _____

2. _____   7. _____

3. _____   8. _____

4. _____   9. _____

5. _____   10. _____

ACTIVITY 6.11: Bop-It (Optional)

OBJECTIVE: Students will learn to follow oral directions by playing the game Bop-It.

MATERIALS: Bop-It Game

PROCEDURES:

1. Have students form a circle.

2. Tell the students that they are going play the game Bop-It. Ask the students what kind of directions will they be following. They will follow oral directions.

3. Show the students how the game works by playing it once. Tell them that the game will give them an oral direction to follow. Depending on the game you get, it will tell you to pull it, twist it, spin it, or Bop-It. The students must do it quickly or the game will buzz. If that happens, just have the next student start the game again.

4. Discussion questions:

- What was difficult about this game?

- Did you get better or worse the more you played it?

- For some of you who have the game at home, how did you do the first time you played it? (The game probably buzzed more at the beginning, but after practicing they got better).

- How can this game help you follow oral directions in class? (The more you practice at listening, the better you will get).

SUMMARY: Remind the students that it takes practice listening and following oral directions. The students must PAY ATTENTION and think about what was said before doing the task.

Practice

Overview: Practicing is the key to becoming a successful student. Just like the professional athlete must practice to win, students must practice to do well in school. Students can keep their space free from distractions. They can have all the right tools. They can even set goals, PAY ATTENTION in class, and follow directions. But they must study to do well. In this section you will find a variety of strategies and techniques to help students remember and learn the information. As the old saying states, "Practice Makes Perfect."

PRACTICE Contents:

PRACTICE Parent Letter (Included on CD)

Core Lesson 7: "P"- PRACTICE

Activity 7.1 • What is My Learning Style?

Activity 7.2 • Solar System Flashcards

Activity 7.3 • Mnemonic 7

Activity 7.4 • SQ3R

Activity 7.5 • The Frog in the Pool Story

Activity 7.6 • Test-Wise Students

Activity 7.7 • PRACTICE Study Strategies

Optional Activity 7.8 • Wilma Unlimited Book

CORE LESSON 7: "P" – Practice

OBJECTIVE: Students will learn that practicing is an important study habit in order to be successful.

MATERIALS: Pictures printed out of Olympic or professional athletes, musicians, scientists, etc. (three or four). (Examples are Michael Jordan, Jack Nicholson, Gabby Douglas, Thomas Edison, Aretha Franklin). Optional items: Ping pong balls, plastic cups , sheets of paper and a small bucket

PROCEDURES:

1. Draw the steps on the board like Picture A below. Review letters "S," "T," "E," "P" and "U" by asking students what they remember about each letter and why they are important study habits.

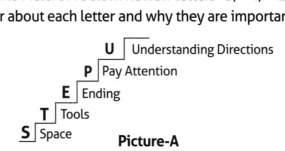

2. Introduce the last letter "P" by writing the letter "P" on the next step and the word PRACTICE by it like Picture B below. Ask students what it means to PRACTICE.

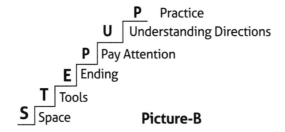

3. Ask the students if they have ever heard these quotes:

   • Practice makes perfect

   • A little practice goes a long way

   • How do you get to Carnegie Hall? Practice, Practice, Practice

   Ask the students what they think those quotes mean.

4. Ask students if they have ever heard of the 10,000 rule. Tell the students that in a book called the *Outliers: The Story of Success* by Malcolm Gladwell he mentions that it takes 10,000 hours of practice to achieve mastery in a given field. He mentions that Bill Gates, the founder of Microsoft, started programming and practicing on computers at the age of 13. The Beatles played for more than 10,000 hours between 1960 and 1964 which launched them into a successful music career.

CORE LESSON 7: "P" – Practice

CONTINUED...

5. Show students a picture of an Olympic or professional athlete. Ask the students how this person got to where he/she is today. He/she had to practice every day. Ask them if they think this person practiced about 10,000 hours. Show them a couple more pictures.

6. Tell the students that to do well in school they need to practice. Good grades are not just going to come without some effort. They need to make a commitment to do their best. And that means practicing.

7. Ask the students what would happen if they had a social studies test tomorrow and they didn't study. They would probably do poorly. Tell them that grades and being a successful student is up to them. They could practice for their social studies test and do well or not study and do badly. Tell the students that many people who have succeeded in life often felt like not practicing, but they knew what would happen if they did not. Imagine Michael Phelps (Gold Medal Swimmer) if he decided not to practice. He might not have any medals.

8. Ask the students what good grades can do for them after high school. There may be scholarships available for them to go to college. There may be more career opportunities available for them as well.

9. Discuss with the students that everyone learns differently and some subjects may be more difficult for some than others, but it is important to try. Tell them that Stephen Kaggwa said, "Try and Fail, but don't fail to try."

10. Optional Activities:

   A. Distribute one ping pong ball and a plastic cup to each student. Have them practice bouncing the ball into the cup. After a certain amount of time ask the students if they got better with practice.

   B. Divide the class into groups of 4-5 students. Give each group a small bucket (the size of an ice-cream bucket). Have each student wad up five pieces of scrap paper. Tell the students stand a certain length away from a bucket and see how many they can get into the bucket. If there is enough room have all the students toss them at once or take turns. If they take turns each group will only need one set of paper balls. Have them practice to see if they get better.

SUMMARY: Remind the students that to be good at anything in life, they must practice.

ACTIVITY 7.1: What is My Learning Style?

OBJECTIVE: Students will discover how they learn best by identifying their learning style.

MATERIALS: What is My Learning Style worksheet (one for each student), Learning Style Cards (copied and cut apart)

PROCEDURES:

1. Ask students to raise their hand if they like math…if they like reading…if they like science…if they like social studies. Discuss how everyone is different and some students like one subject more than another.

2. Tell the students that we also all learn differently. If we know how we learn best, it can often help us in class and when we study.

3. Distribute What is My Learning Style worksheet to students. Have the students look at the row going across and pick just one that is most like them by checking the box.

4. Once they finish, have them add up the number of checks in each column and write their score at the bottom on the line. Tell the students that their highest score will tell them what kind of learner they are.

5. Discuss the three types of learners:

   AUDITORY LEARNERS: (EARS)
   - Prefer talking to people
   - Enjoy listening to the teacher
   - Prefer to read notes out loud

   VISUAL LEARNERS: (EYES)
   - Prefer seeing information written on the board
   - Enjoy reading about new information
   - Learn better with visual aids

   HANDS-ON LEARNERS: (TOUCHING)
   - Enjoy moving around and touching things
   - Like to doodle or create
   - Prefer using many colors to highlight material

6. Distribute the Auditory Learning Style Card to the students who scored high in that area. Distribute the Visual Learning Style Card to the students who scored high in that area. And the same for the Hands-on learners. Discuss each of the Learning Style Cards. Have the students glue this in their agenda to look back on throughout the year.

SUMMARY: Remind the students that everyone learns differently. Tell them to look at the Learning Style Cards to help them in class and when they are studying at home.

What is My Learning Style?

NAME _____

DIRECTIONS: Pick the statement that best describes you. Check only one box for each row.

AUDITORY LEARNER	VISUAL LEARNER	HANDS-ON LEARNER
☐ I like to listen to the teacher.	☐ I like my teacher to write information on the board.	☐ I like to participate in the lesson the teacher is teaching.
☐ For math, I like my teacher to explain new concepts.	☐ For math, I like to see examples on the board.	☐ For math, I like to use cubes, geo boards, etc. to learn.
☐ I enjoy giving oral book reports.	☐ I like to write book reports.	☐ I like making the posters for my book report.
☐ I prefer my coach telling me how to improve my game.	☐ I like to watch and learn from other players who do well.	☐ I improve most by playing the game.
☐ When I learn something new I like to hear someone talk about it.	☐ I like to read about new things.	☐ I like to learn new things by doing them.
☐ I enjoy listening to books on tape.	☐ I enjoy reading books.	☐ I like to act out stories.
☐ I prefer listening to someone read my study guide out loud.	☐ I learn best by reading my study guide over and over again.	☐ I like to make up songs to help me remember my study guide.
☐ I like to talk with my friends.	☐ I like to watch TV.	☐ I like to play outside.
☐ I like to read information out loud.	☐ I like to picture the information in my mind.	☐ I like to highlight my notes and doodle on my paper.
☐ For spelling words, I like to spell them out loud so I can hear them.	☐ For spelling words, I like to write them down so I can see them.	☐ For spelling words, I like to trace the words with my finger in the air.

_____Total Checks for Column 1 _____Total Checks for Column 2 _____Total Checks for Column 3

Learning Style Cards

AUDITORY LEARNER

- Record your notes or study guide and listen back to them back.
- Read information out loud.
- Ask questions.
- Participate in class discussions. It will help you to remember the information.
- Give an oral presentation if you have the choice.
- Watch and listen to educational videos.
- Avoid any noise distractions.

AUDITORY LEARNER

- Record your notes or study guide and listen to them back.
- Read information out loud.
- Ask questions.
- Participate in class discussions. It will help you to remember the information.
- Give an oral presentation if you have the choice.
- Watch and listen to educational videos.
- Avoid any noise distractions.

VISUAL LEARNER

- Read over notes and study guides.
- Draw charts, graphs, or pictures to help you remember information.
- Take notes.
- Watch educational videos.
- Make flash cards to help you study.
- Highlight information in different colors.
- Copy down information from the board.
- Picture the information in your head.

VISUAL LEARNER

- Read over notes and study guides.
- Draw charts, graphs, or pictures to help you remember information.
- Take notes.
- Watch educational videos.
- Make flash cards to help you study.
- Highlight information in different colors.
- Copy down information from the board.
- Picture the information in your head.

HANDS-ON LEARNER

- Learn best by doing things.
- Use highlighters, colored pencils, and pens to help information stand out.
- Move around while studying.
- Take breaks to avoid becoming restless.
- Make a game out of the material, such as flashcards.
- Squeeze a squish ball while studying.

HANDS-ON LEARNER

- Learn best by doing things.
- Use highlighters, colored pencils, and pens to help information stand out.
- Move around while studying.
- Take breaks to avoid becoming restless.
- Make a game out of the material, such as flashcards.
- Squeeze a squish ball while studying.

ACTIVITY 7.2: Solar System Flashcards

OBJECTIVE: Students will learn to practice studying for a test by using flashcards.

MATERIALS: Solar System Flashcards (copied on cardstock front to back (pg. 1 & 2) and laminated; one set per student put in baggies), Solar System Test (one per student)

PROCEDURES:

1. Ask the students to raise their hand if they have ever made flashcards to study for a test. Tell the students that using flashcards is one of the best ways to study for a test. Sometimes students do not have someone to quiz them so flashcards are the easiest way to practice.

2. Tell the students that they are going to practice studying the terms of the solar system by using flashcards. Distribute Solar System Flashcards to each student.

3. Tell the students that when using flashcards they are to look at the definition and then name the term in their mind. Have them look on the back to see if it was correct. Tell them to make two piles; ones they know and ones they don't know yet. Continue to go over the "Don't Know Yet" pile until they learned them all.

4. Have students practice for about five to ten minutes. Tell them once they mastered looking at the definition and naming the term, have them look at the term and then name the definition. Continue for another five minutes or however long you feel the students need.

5. Collect the baggies of flashcards. Distribute Solar System Test to each student.

6. Have students take the test. Read the answers once they are finished. Discuss how the students only had a short amount of time to practice the terms. Discuss that everyone is different and it may only take a short time for some to learn the science terms where for others it may take longer.

7. Tell the students that this gives them an idea of how to make flashcards and study for a test. Tell them that they did well with the short amount of time to study.

Note: It is best to use current subject material that the students are learning, but often schedules do not concur at the same time as the lesson. Also tell the students that this is practice to show them how to use flashcards. They are not meant to get perfect scores only to see that the more they practice, the more they will know.

SUMMARY: Remind the students to make flashcards using the vocabulary terms from their text books or study guides. Have them keep the flashcards for an end of year review.

Solar System Flashcards

A real or imaginary line
that a spinning object
turns around

The center of our solar
system and the closest
star to earth

A hot glowing sphere of
gases that gives off energy

The biggest and brightest
object in the night sky

An imaginary circle
around earth's surface
that divides the earth into
two hemispheres

The sun and all the objects
that orbit around it

A number of stars that
appears to form a pattern

Chunks of rock and metal
that orbit the sun

Solar System Flashcards Answer Sheet

SUN	AXIS
MOON	STAR
SOLAR SYSTEM	EQUATOR
ASTEROID	CONSTELLATION

Solar System Test

NAME _____

DIRECTIONS: Match the correct vocabulary word with the correct definition by writing the number on the line.

1. SUN	3. SOLAR SYSTEM	5. CONSTELLATION	7. EQUATOR
2. AXIS	4. MOON	6. STAR	8. ASTEROID

A. _____ A hot glowing sphere of gases that gives off energy.

B. _____ The earth turns about on this imaginary line.

C. _____ The biggest and brightest object in the night sky.

D. _____ A number of stars that appears to form a pattern.

E. _____ An imaginary circle around the earth's surface that divides the earth into two hemispheres.

F. _____ Chunks of rock and metal that orbit the sun.

G. _____ The closest star to earth and the center of our solar system.

H. _____ the sun and all the objects that orbit around it.

Solar System Test Answer Sheet

NAME_____

DIRECTIONS: Match the correct vocabulary word with the correct definition by writing the number on the line.

1. SUN	3. SOLAR SYSTEM	5. CONSTELLATION	7. EQUATOR
2. AXIS	4. MOON	6. STAR	8. ASTEROID

A. __6.__ A hot glowing sphere of gases that gives off energy.

B. __2.__ The earth turns about on this imaginary line.

C. __4.__ The biggest and brightest object in the night sky.

D. __5.__ A number of stars that appears to form a pattern.

E. __7.__ An imaginary circle around the earth's surface that divides the earth into two hemispheres.

F. __8.__ Chunks of rock and metal that orbit the sun.

G. __1.__ The closest star to earth and the center of our solar system.

H. __3.__ the sun and all the objects that orbit around it.

ACTIVITY 7.3: Mnemonic 7

• **OBJECTIVE:** Students will learn to practice memorizing a list by using a mnemonic.

MATERIALS: Mnemonic 7 (one for each student), Pencils

PROCEDURES:

1. Tell the students that sometimes they will need to learn a list of information for a test. Write the word "Mnemonic" on the board. Ask the students if they have ever heard of the word "Mnemonic" before. A mnemonic is a learning technique that helps you remember information.

2. Distribute worksheet Mnemonic 7 to each student. Have them complete the pre-test according to the directions. When they are finished give them the answers and have them mark their score.

3. Tell them that they are now going to learn how to make a mnemonic. Write the seven countries of Central America on the board. (Nicaragua, Honduras, Guatemala, Panama, Costa Rica, Belize, and El Salvador). Take the first letter of each word and write it on the board lengthwise.

4. Tell the students that to make a mnemonic they need to make a sentence with these letters. (An example is Nine Happy Gorillas Practiced Catching Eleven Bananas). Tell the students that during a test all you need to remember is the silly sentence. Then the first letter will help them remember the countries.

5. Write the other two lists on the board. Have the students use the back of their paper to create a mnemonic. (You can do this as a class together as well)

   • Biological Classifications: Kingdom, Phylum, Class, Order, Family, Genus, Species
     King Phillip Caught One Frog Gathering Seashells

   • Continents: Asia, Africa, North America, South America, Antarctica, Europe, Australia
     An Ant Saw Nine Alligators Eating Apples

6. Have the students study the mnemonics for a few minutes. Have the students take the post-test using the mnemonics they just learned.

7. Read the answers to the post-test. Ask them to raise their hand if they improved their score from the pre-test. Tell them in just a short time they were able to learn this information by using a mnemonic.

SUMMARY: Remind the students that a mnemonic is a technique they can use to help them remember a list of information.

Mnemonic 7

DIRECTIONS: List the following for each question on the lines below.

PRE-TEST
Total Correct _____

A. Name the seven countries in Central America.

1. _____ 5. _____
2. _____ 6. _____
3. _____ 7. _____
4. _____

B. Name the seven biological classifications.

1. _____ 5. _____
2. _____ 6. _____
3. _____ 7. _____
4. _____

C. Name the seven continents.

1. _____ 5. _____
2. _____ 6. _____
3. _____ 7. _____
4. _____

POST-TEST
Total Correct _____

A. Name the seven countries in Central America.

1. _____ 5. _____
2. _____ 6. _____
3. _____ 7. _____
4. _____

B. Name the seven biological classifications.

1. _____ 5. _____
2. _____ 6. _____
3. _____ 7. _____
4. _____

C. Name the seven continents.

1. _____ 5. _____
2. _____ 6. _____
3. _____ 7. _____
4. _____

ACTIVITY 7.4: SQ3R

OBJECTIVE: Students will learn to use the SQ3R method for reading and retaining new information.

MATERIALS: SQ3R Labels (copied onto Avery Labels 18163; cut apart for each student), Avery Labels 18163 (can be bought from office supply places for a pack of 100 for about $6.00). Student Text Book

PROCEDURES:

1. Preparation: Print SQ3R onto Avery Labels 18163. Cut apart for each student.

2. Have students take out their science or social studies book. Have them open it to a chapter they are working on.

3. Explain that the "S" in SQ3R stands for SURVEY. Have them look through the chapter. Point out titles and headings in various sections. Have them look for graphs, bold words, tables, and pictures. Tell the students that to SURVEY a chapter they are learning what the chapter is about.

4. The "Q" stands for QUESTION. Point to a title or heading and ask a student to turn it into a question. For example if the heading is The Industrial Revolution. The question would be: What is the Industrial Revolution? Go through the rest of the chapter turning the titles, bold words, and headings into questions.

5. The first "R" stands for READ. Have the students read a section of the chapter. While they are reading, have them think about the questions they formed earlier.

6. The second "R" stands for RECITE. Have the students recite back what they read by answering the questions they formed from the headings. Tell the students that this part is where they repeat back what they read.

7. The last "R" stands for REVIEW. Have the students look back in the section to see if they missed anything. Have them answer the questions formed earlier again.

8. Distribute SQ3R Labels to each student. Have them put it in their agenda book where they look at it from time to time.

9. Ask students how this activity will help them PRACTICE what they need to study.

SUMMARY: Remind the students that SQ3R needs to be practiced in order to become a habit. This is an important skills that when learned, will help them to remember information.

SQ3R

Survey: Look at the chapter title and subtitles. Look for pictures, graphs, and tables. What is the chapter about?

Question: Turn the titles and headings into questions.

Read: Read each section for information.

Recite: What was the section about? Answer the questions from above.

Review: Go back over titles, heading, bold words to see if you missed anything.

SQ3R

Survey: Look at the chapter title and subtitles. Look for pictures, graphs, and tables. What is the chapter about?

Question: Turn the titles and headings into questions.

Read: Read each section for information.

Recite: What was the section about? Answer the questions from above.

Review: Go back over titles, heading, bold words to see if you missed anything.

SQ3R

Survey: Look at the chapter title and subtitles. Look for pictures, graphs, and tables. What is the chapter about?

Question: Turn the titles and headings into questions.

Read: Read each section for information.

Recite: What was the section about? Answer the questions from above.

Review: Go back over titles, heading, bold words to see if you missed anything.

SQ3R

Survey: Look at the chapter title and subtitles. Look for pictures, graphs, and tables. What is the chapter about?

Question: Turn the titles and headings into questions.

Read: Read each section for information.

Recite: What was the section about? Answer the questions from above.

Review: Go back over titles, heading, bold words to see if you missed anything.

SQ3R

Survey: Look at the chapter title and subtitles. Look for pictures, graphs, and tables. What is the chapter about?

Question: Turn the titles and headings into questions.

Read: Read each section for information.

Recite: What was the section about? Answer the questions from above.

Review: Go back over titles, heading, bold words to see if you missed anything.

SQ3R

Survey: Look at the chapter title and subtitles. Look for pictures, graphs, and tables. What is the chapter about?

Question: Turn the titles and headings into questions.

Read: Read each section for information.

Recite: What was the section about? Answer the questions from above.

Review: Go back over titles, heading, bold words to see if you missed anything.

SQ3R

Survey: Look at the chapter title and subtitles. Look for pictures, graphs, and tables. What is the chapter about?

Question: Turn the titles and headings into questions.

Read: Read each section for information.

Recite: What was the section about? Answer the questions from above.

Review: Go back over titles, heading, bold words to see if you missed anything.

SQ3R

Survey: Look at the chapter title and subtitles. Look for pictures, graphs, and tables. What is the chapter about?

Question: Turn the titles and headings into questions.

Read: Read each section for information.

Recite: What was the section about? Answer the questions from above.

Review: Go back over titles, heading, bold words to see if you missed anything.

SQ3R

Survey: Look at the chapter title and subtitles. Look for pictures, graphs, and tables. What is the chapter about?

Question: Turn the titles and headings into questions.

Read: Read each section for information.

Recite: What was the section about? Answer the questions from above.

Review: Go back over titles, heading, bold words to see if you missed anything.

SQ3R

Survey: Look at the chapter title and subtitles. Look for pictures, graphs, and tables. What is the chapter about?

Question: Turn the titles and headings into questions.

Read: Read each section for information.

Recite: What was the section about? Answer the questions from above.

Review: Go back over titles, heading, bold words to see if you missed anything.

ACTIVITY 7.5: The Frog in the Pool

OBJECTIVE: Students will learn to practice reading comprehension strategies.

MATERIALS: The Frog in the Pool Story and The Frog in the Pool Questions (copied front to back for each student), Highlighter, Pencil

PROCEDURES:

1. Distribute The Frog in the Pool worksheet to each student.

2. Ask the students if this type of test looks familiar. Tell them that they should be used to seeing these when they take reading tests or standardized tests. Tell them that today they are going to learn some strategies that will help with these types of tests.

3. Have the students look at the comprehension questions side first. As a class look at the title of the story. Ask the students based on the title what they think this passage is about. As a class read the questions out loud. Tell the students that reading the questions first will help them when they read the story.

4. Have the students read The Frog in the Pool passage. Tell them when they are reading to take a highlighter or pencil and underline the parts of the story they remember from reading the questions.

5. Have the students answer the comprehension questions. Remind the students to look back at the story if they are not sure about an answer. Discuss the answers.

The Frog in the Pool Answer Key	
1. b	6. c
2. d	7. d
3. c	8. b
4. a	9. a
5. b	10. c

SUMMARY: Remind the students that when they have a reading test to look at the title first, read the questions, and then read the passage. These strategies will help them when answering the comprehension questions.

The Frog in the Pool

It was a beautiful sunny summer day in June just around sunset. The maple trees in the backyard were so green that you would have thought someone painted them they were so perfect. And the smell of the gardenia bushes filled the air with that sweet scent that I wished I could bottle.

I loved to lay in the hammock by the pool at this time of night listening to the crickets sing. The temperature had cooled off just enough that it was very pleasant outside; not too hot and not too cold. I was lying there with my eyes closed, enjoying the sounds of nature, when I heard a strange noise coming from the pool. I ignored it at first, but then it came again. So I went over to the pool and peered over the edge. There on a maple leaf, one that had fallen into the pool, was a frog lying on his back looking up at the sky. He looked up at me and said, "Lovely night, isn't it?" Startled by the sound of a talking frog I didn't know what to say. So I looked around to see if I really heard that.

When I looked back he said, "Yes, I am talking to you. Haven't you ever seen a talking frog before?" "Ah, no.," I said. "Mr. Clover at your service." he said. Still in shock I said, "So you really are a talking frog. How is that so?" "Well, about a year ago I came into your backyard. I had been traveling up the coast heading for the mountains when I saw it; trees so green and inviting that they reminded me of my home back at the pond. And then there was this sweet smell in the air, unlike anything I had ever smelled. So I just had to take a look. As I hopped through the picket white fence and over by the trees, that was when I saw it; a pond so clear that I could see all the way to the bottom. The ponds back home are so murky you can only see about an inch in front of your face. Well I started swimming in your pond every day and lounging by the sweet smelling bushes at night. I would climb up the maple tree during the day and chew off a perfect sized leaf for floating on and then just when the stars popped out I would relax under the bush until morning."

"So you were the one putting maple leaves in the pool. I was wondering how they got in there." I said. "Oh, so that is what you call this; a pool!" he exclaimed. "I thought this was a magic pond." "A magic pond?" I said. "Yes! After a few weeks of swimming in this...what did you call it again? Oh that's right, a pool. It was after a few weeks of swimming in the pool that I started to feel funny. My hearing started to change and my tastes changed too. I couldn't understand the croaking of other frogs nearby and the thought of eating bugs repulsed me." "So it was something in the pool that made you talk?" I said. "Either that or the petals I ate from the sweet smelling bushes." he wondered. "The gardenia bushes?" I said. "Yes, that is it! It was the gardenia bushes!" I exclaimed. "I bought this miracle food to put on the bushes to help them grow." I said. "Wow! It certainly is a miracle food!" "It certainly is!" he said.

Croak! Croak! Croak! My eyes opened suddenly and I quickly looked around. "Where am I?" I thought. I must have fallen asleep. Croak! Croak! Croak! I got up and went over by the pool. There on a maple leaf sat a tiny frog. Croak! Croak! Croak! What a strange dream I had.

The Frog in the Pool Comprehension Questions

DIRECTIONS: Circle the best answer. You may look back at the story.

1. What time of year did the story take place?
    a. Fall   c. Winter
    b. Summer   d. Spring

2. Who is Mr. Clover?
    a. The neighbor   c. A school teacher
    b. A dog   d. A frog

3. What happened first in the story?
    a. Sounds were coming from the pool   c. Listening to the crickets sing
    b. Mr. Clover climbed the maple tree   d. Relaxing under the gardenia bush

4. What was unique about Mr. Clover?
    a. He could talk   c. He could climb trees
    b. He could swim   d. He could walk

5. What is a synonym for the word murky?
    a. Clear   c. Silly
    b. Cloudy   d. Rough

6. What did Mr. Clover do that caused him to talk?
    a. He swam in the pool   c. He ate the gardenia bush pedals
    b. He ate the miracle food   d. He chewed off a maple leaf

7. Where was Mr. Clover heading in his travels?
    a. To the beach   c. To the pond
    b. Back home   d. To the mountains

8. What repulsed Mr. Clover?
    a. The sound of crickets chirping   c. The smell of the gardenia bushes
    b. Eating bugs   d. The green maple leaves

9. What looked like they were painted?
    a. The leaves on the maple tree   c. The fence
    b. The gardenia bush   d. The clear blue pool

10. The story of the talking frog in the pool was:
    a. A true story   c. A dream
    b. A story about frogs   d. A non-fiction story

ACTIVITY 7.6: Test-Wise Students

OBJECTIVE: Students will learn test taking strategies.

MATERIALS: Test-Wise Power Point (included on CD), Test-Wise Answer Sheet (one for each student)

PROCEDURES:

1. Distribute the Test-Wise Answer Sheet to each student.

2. Tell the students that they are going to be answering some questions about test taking strategies. A question will appear on the screen. They will have a few seconds to bubble in the correct answer.

3. Tell the students that the correct answer will appear next on the screen. If they get the answer wrong, have them to make a check mark over the question number. At the end of the test they will count up how many they got correct and mark it in the corner.

4. Show the Test-Wise Power Point. Discuss each question.

SUMMARY: Remind the students to make flashcards using the vocabulary terms from their text books or study guides. Have them keep the flashcards for an end of year review.

Test-Wise Students Answer Sheet

NAME _____   Total Correct _____

DIRECTIONS: Bubble in the correct answer.

1. ○ a   ○ b   ○ c   ○ d
2. ○ a   ○ b   ○ c   ○ d
3. ○ a   ○ b   ○ c   ○ d
4. ○ a   ○ b   ○ c   ○ d
5. ○ a   ○ b   ○ c   ○ d
6. ○ a   ○ b   ○ c   ○ d
7. ○ a   ○ b   ○ c   ○ d
8. ○ a   ○ b   ○ c   ○ d
9. ○ a   ○ b   ○ c   ○ d
10. ○ a   ○ b   ○ c   ○ d
11. ○ a   ○ b   ○ c   ○ d
12. ○ a   ○ b   ○ c   ○ d
13. ○ a   ○ b   ○ c   ○ d
14. ○ a   ○ b   ○ c   ○ d
15. ○ a   ○ b   ○ c   ○ d
16. ○ a   ○ b   ○ c   ○ d
17. ○ a   ○ b   ○ c   ○ d
18. ○ a   ○ b   ○ c   ○ d
19. ○ a   ○ b   ○ c   ○ d
20. ○ a   ○ b   ○ c   ○ d

ACTIVITY 7.7: Study Strategies

OBJECTIVE: Students will learn a variety of different study strategies to help them learn.

MATERIALS: PRACTICE Study Strategies Power Point (included on CD), PRACTICE Study Strategy Cards (cut apart for each student)

PROCEDURES:

1. Tell the students that they will be learning several PRACTICE study strategies to help them remember and learn information (Note: If you have already covered some of the strategies in the previous activities then review those in addition to the new ones).

2. Show PRACTICE Study Strategies Power Point. Go through each slide discussing each study strategy.

3. You can choose to just discuss these strategies or create examples for the students to do to go along with them.

4. Once you have finished the power point, distribute the PRACTICE Study Strategy Cards to each student. These can be printed on cardstock or regular paper and then glued in an agenda or binder.

SUMMARY: Remind the students to look at the PRACTICE Study Strategies Card to help them study and learn new information.

PRACTICE Study Strategy Cards

PRACTICE STUDY STRATEGIES
1. Flashcards
2. SQ3R
3. Mnemonics
4. Highlight and Underline
5. Learning Styles
6. Draw it
7. Fold and Check
8. Using your Senses
9. Graphic Organizers
10. Outlining
11. Study Guides

PRACTICE STUDY STRATEGIES
1. Flashcards
2. SQ3R
3. Mnemonics
4. Highlight and Underline
5. Learning Styles
6. Draw it
7. Fold and Check
8. Using your Senses
9. Graphic Organizers
10. Outlining
11. Study Guides

PRACTICE STUDY STRATEGIES
1. Flashcards
2. SQ3R
3. Mnemonics
4. Highlight and Underline
5. Learning Styles
6. Draw it
7. Fold and Check
8. Using your Senses
9. Graphic Organizers
10. Outlining
11. Study Guides

PRACTICE STUDY STRATEGIES
1. Flashcards
2. SQ3R
3. Mnemonics
4. Highlight and Underline
5. Learning Styles
6. Draw it
7. Fold and Check
8. Using your Senses
9. Graphic Organizers
10. Outlining
11. Study Guides

PRACTICE STUDY STRATEGIES
1. Flashcards
2. SQ3R
3. Mnemonics
4. Highlight and Underline
5. Learning Styles
6. Draw it
7. Fold and Check
8. Using your Senses
9. Graphic Organizers
10. Outlining
11. Study Guides

PRACTICE STUDY STRATEGIES
1. Flashcards
2. SQ3R
3. Mnemonics
4. Highlight and Underline
5. Learning Styles
6. Draw it
7. Fold and Check
8. Using your Senses
9. Graphic Organizers
10. Outlining
11. Study Guides

PRACTICE STUDY STRATEGIES
1. Flashcards
2. SQ3R
3. Mnemonics
4. Highlight and Underline
5. Learning Styles
6. Draw it
7. Fold and Check
8. Using your Senses
9. Graphic Organizers
10. Outlining
11. Study Guides

PRACTICE STUDY STRATEGIES
1. Flashcards
2. SQ3R
3. Mnemonics
4. Highlight and Underline
5. Learning Styles
6. Draw it
7. Fold and Check
8. Using your Senses
9. Graphic Organizers
10. Outlining
11. Study Guides

ACTIVITY 7.8: *Wilma Unlimited* (Optional)

OBJECTIVE: Students will learn through the story *Wilma Unlimited* that practice makes a difference.

MATERIALS: Book – *Wilma Unlimited* by Kathleen Krull and Illustrated by David Diaz. ISBN #: 0-15-201267-2. This book can be found through Voyager books or on Amazon.com for $6.00 paperback and $14.00 hardback and *Wilma Unlimited* Worksheet

PROCEDURES:

1. Ask the students what an Olympic athlete has to do to get to the Olympics. They need to practice. Ask them if the athletes ever have to overcome obstacles. Discuss some of the obstacles.
2. Tell the students that you are going to read them a story about a woman named Wilma Rudolph who overcame many obstacles to become an Olympic athlete and the world's fastest runner.
3. Read *Wilma Unlimited*.
4. Discussion questions:
    *   Why did people think she wouldn't survive when she was young? (She only weighed a little over four pounds when she was born and she got sick very easily)
    *   What happened to Wilma when she was five years old? (She developed polio and it twisted her leg)
    *   What did the doctors tell her when she got polio? (Wilma would never walk again)
    *   What did the doctors want her to do to help her leg get stronger? (To practice exercises every day, even if it hurt)
    *   Why couldn't Wilma go to school? (Because she couldn't walk)
    *   After practicing her exercises every day, the doctors gave her a metal brace. This allowed her to go to school. Why was she still not happy? (She saw the kids running and jumping and playing basketball)
    *   What did she do to overcome her sadness? (She kept practicing and practicing her exercises)
    *   What happened at church one Sunday? (She took off her brace and walked down the aisle)
    *   In high school, what did Wilma do that made her happy? (She played basketball and took her team to many victories)
    *   Who was watching her at one of the games and what did he do? (Someone from Tennessee State University who gave her a full athletic scholarship)
    *   Would she have received that scholarship without practicing? (No)
    *   After continuous hard-work, where did she get to go? (The Olympics)
    *   What happened at the Olympics? (She won three gold medals even after twisting her ankle)
    *   What does this story tell you about hard-work, practice, and determination?
5. Distribute *Wilma Unlimited* word search and word scramble to students to complete.
    Word Scramble answers:
    1. Goals   2. Athlete   3. Brave   4. Champion   5. Fast   6. Medal

SUMMARY: Remind the students that it takes practice to achieve your goals. The same holds true with their school work. They need to practice the material if they are to do well.

Wilma Unlimited

NAME _____

DIRECTIONS: Find the words below in the word search puzzle and unscramble the words below.

```
D P R A C T I H C E M O A K E
S E P E R F P E C T H L O B E
A S T O T L S S C A Q Y Z L F
M N W E O O N F R C T M J I Z
B T O D R M O D N Y Q P N X X
I Q U Z L M W L R J Y I J R H
T R N Q D O I P S X A C R H M
I Q Z W R I N N E A Z S M W Q
O H G K V D P R A C T I C E Q
U X I Y W M M B Z T A M L I W
S N Y Z M L U G N D I R Q E Q
G Q N O V Q E U V S Y O X M Z
E C N E T S I S R E P Q N N S
G E Z I S L R Z S M O Q F V A
V C F B M A E R D N W K J H Q
```

AMBITIOUS	DETERMINATION	DREAM
HARDWORKING	OLYMPICS	PERSISTENCE
PRACTICE	RUDOLPH	TOOLS
	WILMA	

WORD SCRAMBLE:

1. LAGOS _____

2. LETTHAE _____

3. VERBA _____

4. PINCHMAO _____

5. TAFS _____

6. DEALM _____

Wrap Up

Overview: Developing strong study habits is the key to achieving academic success in school. It is these habits that will then carry on throughout a person's life and into the world of post-secondary work. In this section, students will review "S" for SPACE, "T" for TOOLS, "E" for ENDING, "P" for PAY ATTENTION, "U" for UNDERSTAND DIRECTIONS, and "P" for PRACTICE.

STEP-UP Review Contents:

STEP-UP to Better Grades Review Parent Letter (included on CD)

Core Lesson 8: STEP-UP Wrap-Up

Activity 8.1 • STEP-UP Study Skills Post-test

Activity 8.2 • STEP-UP to Better Grades Bookmarks

Activity 8.3 • STEP-UP Top 3 Game

Activity 8.4 • Good and Bad Study Habits

Activity 8.5 • Name that Habit

CORE LESSON 8: STEP-UP Wrap-Up

OBJECTIVE: Students will review the letters S T E P U P and their importance.

MATERIALS: Paper, Pencils

PROCEDURES:

1. Tell the students that this is the completion of the STEP-UP for Better Grades program.
2. Divide the class into six groups. Assign each group a letter from STEP-UP. (One group will have the letter "S," another will have the letter "T," and so on).

   S- SPACE

   T- TOOLS

   E- ENDING

   P- PAY ATTENTION

   U-UNDERSTAND DIRECTIONS

   P- PRACTICE

3. Distribute paper and pencils to each group. Tell the students that they will have about five minutes to write down everything they can remember about their assigned letter.

4. Have each group present to the class on the following questions:
   • What are the key points for your assigned letter?
   • What makes these key points important?
   • How does this letter (habit) help you to be successful in school?

5. When a group finishes, ask the audience if they remember any additional key points to the letter they discussed.

SUMMARY: Ask students what helped them the most throughout these sessions.

ACTIVITY 8.1: STEP-UP Study Skills Post-Test

OBJECTIVE: Students will review the study skills areas that they improved upon in school and at home.

MATERIALS: STEP-UP Study Skills Post-test, STEP-UP Study Skills Pre-test (from first session), STEP-UP Study Skills Goal Sheet (cut apart)

PROCEDURES:

1. Distribute STEP-UP Study Skills Post-test to all students.

2. Tell students that they will read each statement and circle either 5= Always, 4= Often, 3= Sometimes, 2= Rarely or 1= Never for how that statement pertains to them.

3. Once students are finished, have them score their post-test by adding up the numbers they circled.

4. Discuss post-test statements and the scores.
   - 30+ Excellent – Great working skills
   - 25-29 Good – Need help in a few areas
   - <24 Improvements needed- Talk to your counselor or teacher for some assistance

5. Distribute pre-tests to students from the first session. Ask them if they improved. Ask them how they did with the goals they wrote down during that lesson.

6. Optional: Distribute STEP-UP Study Skills Goal Sheet to each student. Ask them to continue with their current goals or write down two new goals that they would like to work on for the rest of the school year.

SUMMARY: Remind students that even when they think they know what to do, it is still important to read the directions to make sure they are following the instructions correctly.

STEP-UP Study Skills Post-test

NAME _____

DIRECTIONS: Please circle the number that applies to you for each statement.

1 = Never   2 = Rarely   3 = Sometimes   4 = Often   5 = Always

1. I have a quiet place at home to do my work.   1 2 3 4 5

2. I bring all necessary materials to class; paper and pencils.   1 2 3 4 5

3. I plan out all of my projects and assignments so I am not rushed
before they are due.   1 2 3 4 5

4. I PAY ATTENTION in class.   1 2 3 4 5

5. I follow directions in class the first time given.   1 2 3 4 5

6. I hand assignments in on time.   1 2 3 4 5

7. I study for my tests using different techniques.   1 2 3 4 5

Add the numbers from each statement to get a total score.   Total Score _____

Total score results:

30+ Excellent – Great working skills

25-29 Good – Need help in a few areas

< 24 Improvements needed – Talk to teachers or your school counselor for some assistance

MY STEP-UP STUDY SKILLS GOALS ARE:

1._____

2._____

MY STEP-UP STUDY SKILLS GOALS ARE:

1._____

2._____

MY STEP-UP STUDY SKILLS GOALS ARE:

1._____

2._____

MY STEP-UP STUDY SKILLS GOALS ARE:

1._____

2._____

MY STEP-UP STUDY SKILLS GOALS ARE:

1._____

2._____

MY STEP-UP STUDY SKILLS GOALS ARE:

1._____

2._____

MY STEP-UP STUDY SKILLS GOALS ARE:

1._____

2._____

MY STEP-UP STUDY SKILLS GOALS ARE:

1._____

2._____

ACTIVITY 8.2: STEP-UP To Better Grades Bookmarks

OBJECTIVE: Students will be reminded of the STEP-UP to Better Grades study habits and skills by making bookmarks.

MATERIALS: STEP-UP to Better Grades Bookmarks (copied on cardstock and cut apart for each student), Art Supplies (Crayons, colored pencils, or markers)

PROCEDURES:

1. Put the steps on the board with the letters STEP-UP like Picture A below. Ask the students what each letter stands for in STEP-UP to Better Grades.

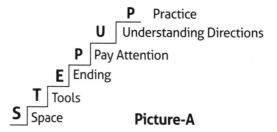

Picture-A

P Practice
U Understanding Directions
P Pay Attention
E Ending
T Tools
S Space

2. Review each letter by asking the students what they remember about each habit they learned.

   • **S-SPACE**: Students must be responsible for where they study at home. They must have a space that is free from distractions. The TV should be off and electronics put away. Students should sit at a table or desk and have enough light to do homework.

   • **T-TOOLS**: In order to stay organized it is important to have the correct tools as a student. The two most important tools of a student are an agenda book and a homework folder. Students should also have a toolbox nearby at home so they do not have to get up to look for needed supplies.

   • **E-ENDING**: Students must plan out long term projects. They must start at the beginning to get to the ending. Students must also prioritize their school work by setting short-term goals.

   • **P-PAY ATTENTION**: Students should keep their eyes on the teacher and listen carefully in class.

   • **U-UNDERSTAND DIRECTIONS**: It is important to carefully follow oral and written directions.

   • **P-PRACTICE**: Just like professional athletes must practice to get better, students must practice to do well in school. It is also important to use a variety of study strategies to learn the information.

3. Distribute STEP-UP to Better Grades Bookmarks to each student. Have the students color them. They can keep them the way they are or laminate them.

SUMMARY: Ask students to use their Bookmarks so they can be reminded of the STEP-UP to Better Grades Study Habits.

STEP-UP Bookmarks

STEP-UP TO BETTER GRADES

S–SPACE: Be responsible about your space. Eliminate distractions.

T–TOOLS: Stay organized. Use your agenda daily.

E–ENDING: Set goals and break down big projects.

P–PAY ATTENTION: Listen carefully in class.

U–UNDERSTAND DIRECTIONS: Follow written and oral directions carefully.

P–PRACTICE: You must study or practice to learn the information.

STEP-UP TO BETTER GRADES

S–SPACE: Be responsible about your space. Eliminate distractions.

T–TOOLS: Stay organized. Use your agenda daily.

E–ENDING: Set goals and break down big projects.

P–PAY ATTENTION: Listen carefully in class.

U–UNDERSTAND DIRECTIONS: Follow written and oral directions carefully.

P–PRACTICE: You must study or practice to learn the information.

STEP-UP TO BETTER GRADES

S–SPACE: Be responsible about your space. Eliminate distractions.

T–TOOLS: Stay organized. Use your agenda daily.

E–ENDING: Set goals and break down big projects.

P–PAY ATTENTION: Listen carefully in class.

U–UNDERSTAND DIRECTIONS: Follow written and oral directions carefully.

P–PRACTICE: You must study or practice to learn the information.

STEP-UP TO BETTER GRADES

S–SPACE: Be responsible about your space. Eliminate distractions.

T–TOOLS: Stay organized. Use your agenda daily.

E–ENDING: Set goals and break down big projects.

P–PAY ATTENTION: Listen carefully in class.

U–UNDERSTAND DIRECTIONS: Follow written and oral directions carefully.

P–PRACTICE: You must study or practice to learn the information.

ACTIVITY 8.3: STEP-UP Top 3 Game

OBJECTIVE: Students will review various study habits by working together as a team.

MATERIALS: STEP-UP Top 3 Power Point, Dry-Erase Board and marker (one for each group) (Can use paper and pencil too), Optional: Prizes (pencils, erasers, candy, etc.)

PROCEDURES:

1. Distribute board and marker (or paper and pencil) to each group.

2. Write the number of teams on the board (ex. Team 1, Team 2, Team 3, etc.)

3. Put the first slide of the STEP-UP Top 3 Power Point on the screen. Tell the students that they will be playing a game to review some of the study habits they have learned.

4. Review STEP-UP to Better Grades by going through the slides.

5. How to play the game:
   - Tell the students that a question will show up on the screen. Each team will a few minutes to write down ONLY THREE answers to the question on their board or paper.

   - You will then display the first answer and ask each team if they had that answer on their board or paper. If they did, write down the point value they earned under their team number. Discuss the study habits along the way.

   - Show the next answer on the screen. If a team had that answer, write down the point value they earned under their team number.

   - Continue the same way with the rest of the questions.

   (Hint: While they are writing down the answers to the next question, total up the team points after each question).

6. Optional: Declare a team winner by giving out prizes.

SUMMARY: Ask the students what they learned from this review activity. Ask which habit is their favorite one to use and which one is most difficult.

ACTIVITY 8.4: Good & Bad Study Habits

OBJECTIVE: Students will review good and bad study habits.

MATERIALS: Good and Bad Study Habits sheet (one for each student), Pencils

PROCEDURES:

1. Tell the students that today they are going to review some good and bad study habits.

2. Distribute Good and Bad Study Habits sheet to each student. Tell them that they are to circle all the good study habits and put an X on all the bad study habits.

3. When they have finished discuss each good and bad study habit.

SUMMARY: Ask the students why it is important to have good study habits.

Good & Bad Study Habits

NAME _____

DIRECTIONS: Circle all the good study habits and put an X over all the bad study habits below.

Read a book while the teacher is talking

Turn in completed homework to your teacher

Ask for help if you need it

Read written direction 2-3 times

Use flashcards to help you study

Get plenty of rest

Forget your homework at home

Keep your eyes on the teacher to help you pay attention

Keep toys in your desk to play with at school

Use your agenda daily

Knowing your learning style will help you learn

Rush through your school work

Leave your agenda blank

Put papers loosely in your desk

Keep a toolbox nearby when doing your homework

Put finished homework in the pocket of your bookbag

Use SQ3R when reading

Do your homework on the bed

Do your homework with the TV on

Do your book report the night before it is due

Eat a good breakfast every day

Make your study space free from distractions

ACTIVITY 8.5: Name that Habit

OBJECTIVE: Students will review study skills habits by matching each STEP-UP habit with the behavior.

MATERIALS: Name that Habit worksheet (for each student), Name that Habit Key, Pencils

PROCEDURES:

1. Tell the students that they will be reviewing the study habits they learned in the past sessions.

2. Distribute Name that Habit worksheet to each student. Discuss each of the STEP-UP Habits at the top of the page. Ask the students what they remember about each one.

3. You can review as much as you would like by using the information below:
   - **S-SPACE**: Students must be responsible for where they study at home. They must have a space that is free from distractions. The TV should be off and electronics put away. Students should sit at a table or desk and have enough light to do homework.
   - **T-TOOLS**: In order to stay organized it is important to have the correct tools as a student. The two most important tools of a student are an agenda book and a homework folder. Students should also have a toolbox nearby at home so they do not have to get up to look for needed supplies.
   - **E-ENDING**: Students must plan out long term projects. They must start at the beginning to get to the ending. Students must also prioritize their school work by setting short-term goals.
   - **P-PAY ATTENTION**: Students should keep their eyes on the teacher and listen carefully in class.
   - **U-UNDERSTAND DIRECTIONS**: It is important to carefully follow oral and written directions.
   - **P-PRACTICE**: Just like professional athletes must practice to get better, students must practice to do well in school. It is also important to use a variety of study strategies to learn the information.

4. Have the students match the habit at the top of the page with the statement by writing the correct letter on the line below.

5. When the students have finished, read off the answers by using the key. Discuss the statements.

SUMMARY: Have students check off each of the habits they currently practice. Ask students what new habits have they learned that will help them succeed in school.

Name that Habit Worksheet

NAME _____

DIRECTIONS: Write the correct letter next to the statement below.

S- SPACE	**PA- PAY ATTENTION**
T- TOOLS	**U- UNDERSTAND DIRECTIONS**
E- ENDING	**P- PRACTICE**

1. _____ Using SQ3R will help you learn what you read.

2. _____ Keeping the TV off will help you focus while doing your homework.

3. _____ It is important to break down projects into smaller steps.

4. _____ Keep your eyes on the teacher to stay focused in class.

5. _____ You use your ears to follow oral directions.

6. _____ Using your agenda will help you stay organized.

7. _____ Highlighting and underlining will help you learn key points.

8. _____ It is important when doing your homework to keep your area free from distractions.

9. _____ Listening to the teacher will help you do well in school.

10. _____ It is important to set goals at school.

11. _____ Use your eyes to follow written directions.

12. _____ Keep a toolbox nearby when you are doing your homework to keep you from getting up.

13. _____ Use flashcards to help you study for tests.

14. _____ It is helpful to plan out and write due dates on a calendar.

15. _____ The homework folder will help you keep your homework from getting lost.

Name that Habit Key

NAME _____

DIRECTIONS: Write the correct letter next to the statement below.

S- SPACE   PA- PAY ATTENTION
T- TOOLS   U- UNDERSTAND DIRECTIONS
E- ENDING   P- PRACTICE

1. __P__ Using SQ3R will help you learn what you read.

2. __S__ Keeping the TV off will help you focus while doing your homework.

3. __E__ It is important to break down projects into smaller steps.

4. __PA__ Keep your eyes on the teacher to stay focused in class.

5. __U__ You use your ears to follow oral directions.

6. __T__ Using your agenda will help you stay organized.

7. __P__ Highlighting and underlining will help you learn key points.

8. __S__ It is important when doing your homework to keep your area free from distractions.

9. __PA__ Listening to the teacher will help you do well in school.

10. __E__ It is important to set goals at school.

11. __U__ Use your eyes to follow written directions.

12. __T__ Keep a toolbox nearby when you are doing your homework to keep you from getting up.

13. __P__ Use flashcards to help you study for tests.

14. __E__ It is helpful to plan out and write due dates on a calendar.

15. __T__ The homework folder will help you keep your homework from getting lost.

About the Author

Robin Zorn has been named the 2014 National School Counselor of the Year. As a Professional School Counselor since 1994, she has presented numerous times locally, state-wide, and nationally on topics such as Collaboration: Keeping Students from Falling through the Cracks – An Essential Piece to RTI (Response to Intervention), the ASCA National Model, Goals of Misbehavior, Legislative Issues in School Counseling, Character Education, and her well known STEP-UP to Better Grades Curriculum. She has held several leadership positions on the local and state levels where she has served as the 2nd VP for the Georgia School Counseling Association, the ASCA Model/Career Development Chair, and the 21st Century Comprehensive Counseling Co-coordinator for Gwinnett County. Robin is most known locally for implementing the successful county wide Elementary School Peer Leadership Conference and the innovative program called Girl PRIDE – a mentoring program for 5th grade girls. She was also recognized in Gwinnett County for developing the best practices for meeting the elementary school college and career requirements in Georgia. Robin received her M.Ed and Ed.S school counseling degrees from Georgia State University and she is also certified in 7-12 social studies and is trained as a play therapist. Robin enjoys collaborating with her husband, who is a middle school counselor, going to Jazzercise, reading, traveling, playing tennis, and spending time with her two teenage daughters.